The Knowledge Context

Comparative Perspectives on
The Distribution of Knowledge

Philip G. Altbach

State University of New York Press

Published by
State University of New York Press, Albany

Printed in the United States of America

For information, address State University of New York Press, State University Plaza, Albany, N.Y., 12246

Library of Congress Cataloging in Publication Data

Altbach, Philip G.
The knowledge context.

Includes index.
1. Publishers and publishing—Developing countries.
2. Book industries and trade—Developing countries.
3. Learning and scholarship—Developing countries.
4. Books and reading—Developing countries.
5. Developing countries—Intellectual life. I. Title.
Z289.A47 1987 070.5′09172′4 86-19167
ISBN 0-88706-444-2
ISBN 0-88706-445-0 (pbk.)

10 9 8 7 6 5 4 3 2 1

Contents

Foreword

The Knowledge Context reflects more than a decade of research and analysis relating to publishing and knowledge dissemination, much of it concerning the Third World. My first research on this topic, which resulted in *Publishing in India: An Analysis,* was stimulated by a fascination with the lively and flourishing publishing scene in India.[1] That research led to reflections on the international implications of book and journal publishing and especially on the relationships between the Third World and the industrialized nations. In 1977, I began a kind of practical internship in publishing as advisory editor to the Praeger Publishers Comparative Education Series and a year later as editor of the *Comparative Education Review,* published by the University of Chicago Press. These editorial responsibilities permitted me to work within the publishing industry and to be directly involved in decision making. I also had the opportunity to serve as a consultant on publications to the Regional Institute of Higher Education and Development in Singapore and to closely observe the development of scholarly and journal publishing in Southeast Asia. Thus, this volume reflects a combination of research and experience as well as an overarching concern with the relationships between the industrialized nations of the North and the less developed countries South in a world of both inequality and interdependence.

The essays in this volume have been published in other formats, sometimes in different versions. I would like to acknowledge the following journals and publishers, all of whom have generously granted their permission so that the essays can appear here:

Chapter 1 is reprinted from the *Annals of the American Academy of Political and Social Science* 421 (September 1975), pp. 1–13.

Chapter 2 is reprinted from *Harvard Educational Review* 45 (May 1975), pp. 226–236 (copyright by the President and Fellows of Harvard College).

Chapter 3 is reprinted from *Library Trends* 26 (Spring 1978), pp. 489–503.

Chapter 4 is reprinted from *International Social Science Journal* 37, no. 1 (1985), pp. 109–118 (copyright by UNESCO).

Chapter 5 is published in this volume for the first time.

Chapter 6 was prepared for a seminar on textbook production in the Third World organized by the World Bank in Washington, D.C., April 1986. It is printed here with the permission of the World Bank.

Chapter 7 is reprinted from *Prospects* 13, no. 1 (1983), pp. 315–325 (copyright by UNESCO).

Chapter 8 is reprinted from *Scholarly Publishing* 16 (April 1985), pp. 211–222.

Chapter 9 is reprinted from *International Social Science Journal* 31, no. 2 (1979), pp. 328–340 (copyright by UNESCO).

Chapter 10 is reprinted from *Scholarly Publishing* 17 (April 1986), pp. 197–208. The coauthor of this article was S. Gopinathan. The chapter is based on a paper given at the International Conference on Access, Equity, and Collaboration in East-West Scholarly Exchanges, Honolulu, Hawaii, December 1985.

I owe many debts in the development of my ideas on the themes reflected in this volume. Professor Edward Shils of the University of Chicago and Cambridge University, a member of my dissertation committee, first stimulated my interest in the role of knowledge in society. Several of my students and colleagues have worked closely with me on topics related to publishing. In particular, Dr. Eva Rathgeber, coauthor with me of *Publishing in the Third World: Trend Report and Bibliography,*[2] and Dr. S. Gopinathan, coauthor of chapter 10 in this volume and coeditor (with A. Arboleda and me) of *Publishing in the Third World: Knowledge and Development,*[3] have been helpful to me and have influenced my thinking. Both have worked with me on the editorial staff of the *Comparative Education Review.* Dr. Sheila Slaughter coedited with me *Perspectives on Publishing.*[4] Finally, Dr. Gail Kelly has been my colleague at SUNY-Buffalo for the past decade and has collaborated with me on many projects. I am also indebted to the many publishers and editors in the Third World who have been kind enough to offer their insights and comments. In this respect, Samuel Israel of the National Book Trust, India; Narendra Kumar of Vikas Publishers, New Delhi; Tejeshwar Singh of Sage-India; Sujit Mukherjee of Orient-Longmans; and Sadanand and Ramdas Bhatkal of Popular Prakashan, Bombay, have been particularly influential. The research in this volume is part of the work of the Comparative Education Center, State University of New York at Buffalo.

Philip G. Altbach

Introduction

Knowledge in the twentieth century is an international commodity. Its creation and distribution are matters of considerable importance for higher education and research, and of increasing importance for modern technological societies. The new computer-based technologies have made knowledge a basic element of contemporary economics. With the development of data bases and a plethora of other means of communication, the distribution of knowledge has also become extremely complex. It is now a major commercial enterprise involving publishers, journals, data bases, communications companies, and a range of other interests.

The educational system is one of the most important consumers and creators of knowledge. At the most basic level, textbooks and curricular materials are an essential part of the dissemination apparatus. At the most advanced levels, knowledge is transmitted by scholarly journals, by research monographs, and, increasingly, by data bases. Educational institutions and the knowledge dissemination network are directly linked and mutually dependent. At every level, educational institutions must be directly served by books, journals, and other written materials. Increasingly, nontext materials such as films and computer programs are becoming important to the dissemination system.

Because of their purchases, their bibliographical control, and their role as a central source of information, libraries are among society's most important institutions for storing and distributing knowledge. It is not an exaggeration to say that scholarly journals could not survive without the libraries—their major purchasers. The role of libraries has become increasingly complex with the development of data bases, schemes for interlibrary loans, and networking. As a key element in the knowledge dissemination system, libraries are also directly affected by publication trends throughout the world. They have had a difficult time keeping up with the explosion of knowledge, which has resulted in an ever expanding number of books and journals as well as of nonprint materials.

Knowledge is increasingly international. Academic and research communities are linked by common interests in a world where communication is technologically relatively simple. The major centers of research and scholarship, which also dominate the knowledge dissemination system, have worldwide influence. The increasing use of English as the major language of research dissemination and the unquestioned dominance of the scholarly journals published in English is another international reality. The world of scholarship is increasingly one that knows no borders, in which the metropolitan centers of scholarship—largely in North America and Western Europe, and, to a lesser extent, in Eastern Europe—dominate the rest of the world. Multinational publishers are influential in many nations and have a key role in the dissemination apparatus.

This book is concerned with the major themes of the international dissemination of knowledge. It is written in the conviction that the means and structures of dissemination are of critical importance in a world that is increasingly based on knowledge. It is important to understand not only the changing patterns of knowledge dissemination, but also what can be called the "political economy of dissemination"—the patterns of control over the system and the reasons for and implications of that control.

The major international cleavage in knowledge dissemination—the gulf between the power and influence of the major central nations of the Western industrialized world which produce knowledge and the vast hinterland of consuming nations of the Third World, many of which are hardly part of the system at all, is a major theme of this book. I am concerned with exploring the nature of these patterns and their implications for the international knowledge network. While much has been written about elements of the knowledge network—libraries, data bases, or publishers—little attention has been given to the interaction between all of these elements in an international context.

The international diffusion of knowledge is by no means a new phenomenon. Latin was the international language of scholarship in the European Middle Ages, and Arabic and Greek served to preserve much of classical scholarship in a somewhat earlier era. In its sphere,

Chinese held sway over a wide area. But never has a global knowledge system emerged with the technological potential for covering virtually the entire world with networks of communication and dissemination. A few languages with international sway, mainly English, with French, Spanish, and Russian following at some distance, have widespread influence over the dissemination system. Technological advances such as data bases, reprography, and satellite-based communication networks have further contributed to the creation of a global village. This volume is concerned with the implications of these innovations for the complex relationship between the industrialized nations and the Third World.

The essays in this book deal with a number of specific topics, but all are related by an overarching concern for the international implications of the knowledge system. The first section of the book deals with some basic themes of the knowledge network. Essays dealing with the nature of the publishing enterprise, with the specific problems of publishing in the Third World, and with the nature of the knowledge distribution system in India are aimed at providing a broad perspective on the nature of the international system and especially the role of book production and dissemination in that system. This section is also concerned with analyzing the basic inequalities in the system and with the role of dependency and neocolonialism in knowledge distribution, for it is an assumption of this volume that there are dramatic inequalities in the international knowledge system and that in some respects these inequalities are one of the major determining factors in the system.

In the context of these broader concerns, the book proceeds to discuss some important themes in knowledge dissemination as they relate specifically to the Third World. The international copyright system, which has a vast legal literature, has seldom been analyzed from the perspective of how copyright relates to the broader elements of the knowledge system. Copyright, after all, is the nexus of the legal procedures that control the traffic and trade in knowledge throughout the world. The evolution and development of journals in the Third World are also elements in the emergence of an independent knowledge dissemination apparatus that may assist local scientific networks. A consideration of the movement of books from the Third World, in this instance specifically from Southeast Asia, to the industrialized nations is important in providing wider markets for Third

World publications and in ensuring that knowledge travels in both directions and not just from North to South. A discussion of the development of a local publishing industry in the Indian state of Maharashtra illustrates both the problems and the possibilities of indigenous publishing in the Third World.

The main concern of this book is the printed word, which remains the major means for communicating knowledge in educational and research settings. Marshall McLuhan's vision of a video future has not come to pass, at least in education and science, nor does it seem around the corner. Without question, communication through the printed word has undergone many changes in the last few decades. New technologies for composition, printing, and particularly for photocopying have meant major changes for publishers, libraries, and scholars. In some ways, the economics of knowledge dissemination has been altered by these technological changes. But the traditional book and journal remain at the heart of the worldwide dissemination process, despite data bases, library networking, and the ubiquitous photocopying machine. They are likely to remain so for a long time to come, although continuing technological innovations will no doubt continue to stimulate change.

This book is therefore concerned her with the most traditional form of knowledge dissemination—a form which has maintained its basic format since the invention of movable type but which at the same time has undergone massive alteration in economy, scope, and means of distribution. In the modern world, books are produced by some of the largest multinational corporations and also by minipublishers. Both are able to operate successfully. But despite the fact that books can be found in the most remote parts of the world, there are vast disparities in access to reading materials. In many Third World nations, there are such severe shortages of even primary textbooks that most children in school seldom see a textbook. Research libraries, a necessary part of any program of advanced scholarship and research, are largely limited to the major universities in the industrialized nations. This inequality places Third World scientific institutions at an immediate and serious disadvantage. These issues are among the key concerns of this volume.

The chapters of this volume, though seemingly somewhat disparate, are in fact focused around a number of interrelated themes which are of crucial importance for understanding the international knowledge network and especially the nexus of inequalities within that network.

The book deals with some key elements of the technical aspects of publishing and knowledge dissemination. In studying the relationships among nations and among the many elements of the distribution apparatus, it also deals with the political economy of the system. The basic themes of this book are given below.

Centrality. Knowledge distribution, in its manifold forms, is central to contemporary educational systems, to scholarship, and to the diffusion of research. If education and research are to be effective, they must be served by efficient means of disseminating information, usually through books and journals. The centrality of the knowledge distribution apparatus, in all its complexity, is seldom recognized in analyses of educational and research policy.

Internationality. Knowledge is international. Research is disseminated across international borders, and increasingly books and journals have roles beyond their countries of publication. The knowledge system is itself increasingly international in scope. Multinational publishers are common. Journals have circulation in many countries and frequently have editorial boards with scholars from more than one nation. Data bases have an international dissemination capability. Researchers are frequently part of international research teams. In short, the knowledge system has international aspects which are becoming more and more important in economic, political, and research terms.

Inequality. The international knowledge dissemination system is also unequal. It is dominated and controlled by the large, wealthy, and prestigious academic systems, publishers, and research enterprises in the major industrialized nations. Those nations—particularly the United States, Britain, France, the Soviet Union, and, to a lesser extent, West Germany and Japan—are the central intellectual powers of the world, producing most of the world's knowledge and also controlling the means of distributing that knowledge. The smaller industrialized nations are somewhat dependent on these major centers, and the Third World is much more peripheral and dependent on the centers. Thus the balance of intellectual trade is one-sided, with the Third World importing most of its knowledge from the industrialized nations. The location of the major publishers, journals, data bases and producers of computers and software all reinforce this system of inequality. Moreover, the policies of the industrialized nations, as expressed in their foreign aid programs, copyright laws, commercial orientations, and other policies, tend to perpetuate existing inequalities.

Language. The language of publishing and knowledge distribution is important not only for the direct user but also for the broader system of dissemination in the world. The bulk of the world's research and scientific knowledge is disseminated through the major international languages—dominated at present by English, with French, Spanish, and Russian also having some international currency. Most translations are from one of the major international languages into a myriad of smaller tongues. Language is therefore a key element of the international knowledge system, an element that works to the disadvantage of the Third World, which must use one of the metropolitan languages for its access to research and scholarship.

Infrastructure. Knowledge dissemination is a complex, labor-intensive, and intellectually demanding enterprise. Yet it does not require a great deal of money and can be done in a decentralized context. The fact that India has become one of the world's top ten publishing nations with the use of a decidedly "low tech" industry is an indication of the diversity possible in this enterprise. But the trend is toward larger, more capital-intensive and internationally oriented dissemination mechanisms. The creation and development of the basic infrastructures of knowledge dissemination—publishing houses, editors, printing facilities, libraries, and of course a body of writers able to contribute relevant manuscripts—are too often forgotten in the rhetoric of development.

Interrelationships. In a sense, this volume is about interrelationships—symbiotic relationships within a national knowledge system of libraries, educational institutions, scholars and teachers, policymakers, publishers, editors, and of course the reading public. There are also the relationships evident among nations in the international knowledge network, and these relationships are frequently characterized by inequality. But a knowledge network is based on institutions and actors, with each playing an interdependent role. While the international network largely flows from North to South and is dominated by the industrial nations of the North, there are efforts to build ties among the Third World countries in the hope that those ties can produce a greater sense of autonomy.

This volume is concerned with an incredibly complex web of factors that together constitute the worldwide network of knowledge distribution. It is important to understand the nature of a national knowledge system and the specific elements of that system. At the same time, it is necessary to look beyond the national system to the broader international networks and the impact of the international system, with its inherent inequalities, on the national knowledge system. In some ways, the chapters in this book may seem to deal with quite distinct and even diffuse topics, but they are linked by their attempt to understand the nature and implications of knowledge dissemination in the modern world. Although publishing can be seen as part of a broader pattern of social and economic relationships among nations, it can also have some autonomy and independent development.

It is appropriate to conclude on a note of optimism. Just as intellectual creativity knows no international boundaries, so knowledge networks can be established even in poor countries or regions at a distance from the centers of knowledge distribution. It is possible to create an independent publishing enterprise even while elements of the network are linked to trends and policies overseas. Although the publishing industry in the United States has been characterized by mergers and centralization of many of the major firms, at the same time many new smaller publishers have been successfully established to fulfill specific roles. Although these small publishers frequently use the most modern publishing technologies, which frequently do not require massive outlays of capital, yet they function somewhat like cottage industries. By planning carefully, cultivating specific markets, and developing close relations among authors, readers, and institutions such as libraries, these new publishers have a verve and flexibility that the large conglomerates lack. In a sense, their success is based on their ability to work around, rather than against, the dominant forces in the knowledge industry.

Third World publishers also have the potential of building effective knowledge industries which can serve specific local needs and perhaps have a regional relevance within the context of the international networks. Careful planning, sufficient infrastructures, and of course a domestic or regional market that can support books and journals are all necessary. Large expenditures of capital are not required—human skill and a willingness to carve out a niche in an infinitely varied intellectual landscape are the prerequisites. Of course, the challenges are considerable. The "raw materials" of publishing—paper, printing equipment, and the like—are not cheap and are frequently controlled by the industrialized nations. And it is not easy to assemble a cadre of trained personnel able to coordinate the complex process of publishing. It is difficult to ensure an effective national book distribution apparatus and to distribute publications regionally or internationally. Yet these tasks are not beyond the skills and abilities of most Third World nations. Models of the successful development of Third World knowledge industries do exist.

This volume is concerned with describing and analyzing relationships among countries. But an underlying hope is that a deeper and more thorough understanding of the complexity of knowledge networks will lead to the expansion of capabilities in the Third World. The analysis of the inequalities of the international system of knowledge distribution may make those who currently dominate the system more conscious of their responsibilities and may give the dependent nations a sense of the possibilities in the knowledge enterprise. In short, this volume is more than an intellectual exercise—it is an effort to provide an analysis of reality that will lead to change and development. Knowledge, without question, is a key to freedom, development and autonomy. And knowledge distribution is a necessary part of achieving these important goals.

The Knowledge Network

Chapter 1

Publishing and the Intellectual System

Publishing is an integral part of the intellectual and cultural system of any country. This system includes such diverse elements as bookstores, printing establishments, universities, libraries, newspapers, radio, television, and the cinema. In some countries, the intellectual system is highly complex and includes a dense assortment of institutions and agencies with mass audiences. In others, the system is rudimentary and limited to a small, educated minority.

There is also an international aspect to the intellectual system which includes the import and export of books and other mass media, copyright arrangements, and translations. Publishing is only a small part of the intellectual system in most nations, particularly those which are highly industrialized and have a variety of accessible alternatives to books. Publishers compete with the mass media—particularly television—for attention and for a share of the financial returns on the cultural product.

Publishing is part of a complex system of institutions and relationships which are rapidly changing in a world of speedy technological development. The purpose of this chapter is to examine the publishing industry and the way it fits into increasingly complex international networks which oversee the development of intellectual "products" for a society. Since we are primarily concerned with intellectual or knowledge distribution systems, the focus is mainly on scholarly books—volumes which contribute to the total store of knowledge in a culture or to the advancement of such knowledge. Thus, we are concerned with studies in the sciences, social sciences, and humanities; with textbooks, particularly at the post-secondary education levels; and with belles lettres. Popular fiction, comic books, and most other elements of mass culture are not considered. This latter material is very important in any society, but is beyond the scope of this chapter.[1]

Books are not the only means of advancing the so-called high culture of a society. Indeed, traditional printed media are being supplemented increasingly by television and other forms of mass communications as educational and cultural media. Many cultural figures argue that novels and poetry have moved from the center of the creative arts and have been replaced, in part, by film as a medium of expression. Although books no longer hold a monopoly on cultural diffusion, they remain central to the development and distribution of knowledge. Because scholarly works are now one of the most important elements of the book market in terms of contributing to culture and technology, they are the focus of this chapter.

Ancillary to books are journals and magazines. This is especially true for scholarly materials, where journals are a primary means of introducing new materials to specialized readers. Journals also review books and thus are a means of publicizing and criticizing research and analysis. Because of their frequent publication and fairly modest production cost, journals have the advantage of presenting materials quickly and economically to a specific audience.

Despite challenges from other mass media, rising costs, and inherent difficulties of production and distribution, books remain one of the most important means of intellectual communication and continue to be at the center of the intellectual system of most societies. This is perhaps even more true of nations which are not as technologically advanced as the United States.

THE INTELLECTUAL SYSTEM

Books are not published in a vacuum. Publishing is affected directly by many social, economic, and political elements, and by both national and international conditions and trends. The publishing firm is bounded by the physical constraints of production and distribution—for example, labor and transportation, availability of outlets, printing presses, and the cost of paper. The publishing firm must also cope with the complexity of creative and scholarly networks—discovering

Fig. 1. The Book Industry

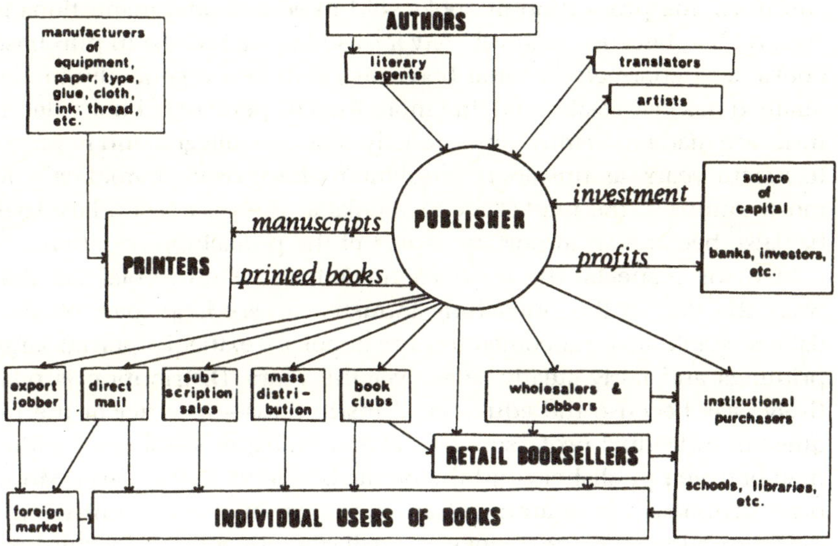

Source: Datus C. Smith, Jr., *A Guide to Book Publishing* (New York: Bowker, 1966).

new talent, pioneering fresh fields, judging the quality and salability of manuscripts, arranging for editing, and working out relationships with individual authors. The publisher is also very much affected by broader social conditions. The nature of the educational system, the condition of libraries and other book purchasing institutions, the rate of literacy in the population, and the accessibility of alternative media all influence publishing. Publishing is vitally important to the intellectual system, but it is only part of a complex network.

The complexity of the intellectual system depends very much on the society of which it is a part. But in almost all countries, the system is complicated and diffuse. Figure 1 diagrams some of the agencies and institutions necessary to bring a book from an author to the reading public.

The educational system is a key consumer of printed materials. In the United States, at least 30 percent of all books sold are textbooks. An additional 11 percent go to libraries, and many libraries are connected with schools and colleges. Elementary and secondary school texts alone account for 16 percent of book sales.[2] In many developing countries, the proportion of books sold to educational institutions is even higher, because relatively few individuals can afford to purchase books, and channels of retail book distribution are generally inadequate. It has been estimated that more than 90 percent of book sales in India are made to institutions—mostly schools, colleges, and libraries. In recent years, as university enrollments have risen dramatically in most countries, the market for textbooks at the post-secondary level has also become an important aspect of the publishing equation.

In many respects, the textbook market is the proverbial tail that wags the dog in the publishing industry; a very large part of publishers' stable income comes from textbooks. Textbooks permit large printings and fairly steady sales over the years. Distribution is relatively easy because the educational institutions—whether at the request of individual professors or curriculum experts—act as middlemen between publishers and the public (students in this case). Moreover, textbooks are guaranteed an audience. In many countries the discount allowed on textbooks is small, thereby allowing publishers maximum profits. It is probably fair to say that without the educational market for books, many publishers could not survive without outside subsidy or control.

Little is known about the ways in which textbooks are selected, or about their authors. Relatively few college texts are written by outstanding scholars, and although publishers often place considerable editorial stress on producing well-written and salable textbooks, standards in many countries, including the United States, are not outstandingly high.[3] Texbook selection processes remain something of a mystery. In a process involving professors, curriculum experts, publishers, editors, and perhaps others, relevant topics are identified and become major areas for textbook emphasis.

In the United States, for example, college and university texts in such areas as black studies, student protest, alternative education, and other fields were stressed for a short time and quickly lost their popularity. Competition for textbook adoption in the United States is sharp, and many alternative books often exist for a single field. The advantage of the American system is that new books that reflect current curricular trends are published quickly. Publishers are eager to meet new curricular demands or to present books which are centered around new teaching materials because more sales are involved.

In fact, many textbooks are commissioned by publishers. They identify areas of current curricular concern and solicit authors to prepare texts in academically popular fields where materials are lacking.

In many countries, where textbook production is less competitive or is in the hands of centralized agencies, books are often less responsive to changing needs. In many developing countries and, of course, in socialist countries, textbook publishing is in the hands of government agencies which have control over what is published and the means of production.

Libraries constitute another key market for books. In the United States, the direct library market is about 11 percent of the total.[4] In developing countries, the library market often constitutes an even larger proportion of the total book market. Libraries are particularly important for certain types of books. For example, about 80 percent of the children's books published in the United States are purchased by libraries. Scholarly books are also very dependent on libraries. In the United States, well over half of the books published by university presses are sold to libraries, and some observers estimate that the proportion is as high as 80 percent. In a Third World country like India, library sales of scholarly books are about 80 to 90 percent. Without library sales, it would be virtually impossible to publish scholarly books. Due to current cutbacks in library budgets in the United States and rising costs for books, and especially for periodicals, it is increasingly difficult for libraries to purchase as many current and scholarly books as in the past.

The existence of journals, book-reviewing media, bibliographies, and other ancillary materials is quite important to publishing and can greatly facilitate the distribution of books and help to create a general "book consciousness" in a society. In addition to acting as an independent outlet for intellectual work, magazines and journals provide a medium for book advertising; perhaps more importantly, they are the key means of reviewing books.

Book reviews are very important for a number of reasons. Reviews publicize books and provide useful information and analysis to potential buyers. Furthermore, reviews contribute to good authorship by criticizing books and subjecting them to public scrutiny. This kind of scrutiny contributes to high levels of intellectual attainment. Many countries do not have adequate book-reviewing media, and this is especially the case for general books.[5] At the level of popular mass market books, reviews in newspapers can contribute to book sales; but in many countries, newspapers do not feature many book reviews.

Bibliographic tools are also an important element of the publishing infrastructure. It is necessary to know about the existence of a book in order to purchase it, and full information concerning its availability and price are also necessary. While most industrialized countries are reasonably well provided with national bibliographies, book-trade journals, and other sources of information, many countries are less well endowed in this respect, and the book trade suffers as a result. Such elements as book-reviewing media and bibliographies are small matters, but they are an integral part of the intellectual system which supports publishing. If they are inadequate, the entire publishing enterprise is weaker.

The rate of literacy in a society is a key variable with regard to publishing. While most industrialized nations have nearly universal literacy and quite high levels of schooling, these countries are a minority. Low literacy rates characterize many Third World nations, and even the minority of individuals who are literate often cannot afford to purchase books. Consequently, book sales are limited, and the publishing enterprise is constricted. In a sense, many Third World publishers are serving only the small minority of their populations that is literate and can afford to buy books. A small audience means limited and costly printings; high costs mean books are available to fewer people. A vicious circle of restricted publishing is created. As a result of these and other factors, the growth of publishing in developing countries has been slow, and intellectual life, the educational system, and other elements of society have suffered.[6]

In addition to literacy, language is often an important issue in publishing. While seldom considered in such linguistically homogeneous nations as the United States, Britain, France, or West Germany, language is a key intellectual, educational, and even political problem in many countries. While particularly acute in the Third World, language is also an issue in such industrialized nations as Belgium, Canada, Yugoslavia, and the Soviet Union. Some countries have competing languages which are used by large minorities of the population. This situation often leads to political strife and conflict and, of course, to a bifurcation of the market for books and to divisiveness in the educational system.

Another aspect of the language problem concerns Third World

countries which continue to use a European language for educational, scientific, and often commercial purposes, despite the fact that this language is spoken by only a small minority of the total population. This situation has implications for many aspects of a society, including levels of political participation and prospects for democracy. For education and publishing, the continued use of a foreign language which is known by only a small proportion of the population (about 2 percent of India's population is literate in English, but about half the books are published in English) necessarily limits the circulation of books and circumscribes the market considerably. Typically, books about politics, science and technology, and other intellectual subjects continue to be written in the European language even after some changes in the linguistic situation occur. Despite the coming of independence and a sense of nationalism in most Third World countries, reliance on written materials in European languages continues to be widespread. Some efforts have been made to establish journals, publish books, and create in general a modern intellectual life in indigenous languages, but progress has been slow. Even Indonesia, which has been particularly active in stressing the use of Bahasa Indonesia as the national language, continues to rely on books from abroad for the higher levels of its educational system.

Publishing also has an international context. Publishers, particularly in the industrialized nations which use a so-called world language, export large quantities of books. Books are also frequently translated from one language to another. The transmission of written materials is a key aspect of intellectual life, and the availability of books to an international audience is important in the international circulation of ideas and technology. Questions of access to books, costs of obtaining permission to translate books, copyright, and commercial arrangements across frontiers are all important to publishers and, indirectly, to intellectual life.

In general, the industrialized nations which use a world language dominate the flow of books and, to considerable extent, the flow of knowledge and ideas as well. In a sense, these nations—especially the United States, Britain, France, and, to a lesser extent, West Germany, Spain, and the Soviet Union—constitute the intellectual centers of the world. Most other nations, and particularly the Third World, are the periphery and are dependent to varying degrees on knowledge, and often books, produced at the center.[7] Some exceptions are the smaller, highly literate nations such as Japan, Sweden, Holland, and Czechoslovakia.

The widespread use of books from abroad has implications for local publishing industries, for the growth of authorship, and for the basic intellectual life of a nation as well. Without an indigenous publishing enterprise, a nation is doomed to a provincial status and will continue to be dependent on outside elements for its intellectual sustenance. The existence of a publishing enterprise does not guarantee an active intellectual life, but publishing is a necessary condition for indigenous scientific and literary activity.

Copyright is a key issue which has international ramifications. Most countries abide by one of the major copyright agreements, and publishers attempt to protect their own interests and those of authors through copyright. Copyright arrangements, however, work in the interests of the major publishing countries and to the detriment of developing nations.[8] After much discussion and controversy, there have been some changes in these agreements which permit developing countries to reprint educational and scientific materials more freely.[9] Copyright regulations control intellectual traffic, and their nature has widespread indirect implications for the shape of the international publishing community.

These are some of the key elements of the intellectual system as it affects publishing. It is not possible in the context of this discussion to evaluate the weights of these and other elements in the system. It is clear, however, that publishing is very much enmeshed in a complex system which extends far beyond the doors of the publishing house. With this broad perspective, let us turn to a more detailed consideration of the internal aspects of publishing.

THE ROLE OF THE PUBLISHER

Most simply, the publisher is a coordinator of the processes by which a book is produced.[10] This coordination, however, requires considerable expertise and the manipulation of many diverse economic, administrative, and intellectual factors. A publisher must understand enough about the market for books that he produces the kinds of books which will be purchased. This is the case even for nonprofit publishers such as university presses. Such publishers need not make a profit, but at the same time they must meet expenses; they cannot issue books which have no attraction even to a scholarly audience. In addition to being economically aware, the publisher must be familiar with the world of arts and letters, science, and social science, and he must hire an editorial staff competent to work in these different arenas. Judgments about the quality, value, and salability of a manuscript must be made constantly.

The publisher must also understand how his product will reach the hands of the intended consumers; he must know the mechanics of the distribution system. The publisher has many roles in an enterprise which is complicated and unpredictable. Even under the best of circumstances, the publishing of so-called serious books is a financially marginal operation.

Lewis Coser has pointed out that the publisher is a "gatekeeper" of knowledge.[11] By virtue of his control over what appears in print, the publisher exercises considerable power. Control over access to information and the means of knowledge distribution is of considerable importance to any society. In most industrialized societies, this control is fairly diffuse, permitting a fairly wide range of material to be published.

Commercial publishers must decide whether a given manuscript has the potential to recoup the investment made on it and hopefully to make a profit. University presses must carefully weigh the scholarly merit of a particular manuscript against its sales potential. If the sales potential is too limited, even the highest-quality manuscript can seldom be published. The means for determining the marketability of a particular book is very unsophisticated.[12] Publishing firms are among the few businesses which rely very little on market research. Thus, the gatekeeping function is often a matter of guesswork. In the case of university presses, committees of established scholars decide whether to publish a manuscript. Such a process maintains an acceptable level of quality but tends to prevent avant-garde or academically unpopular books from being published by university presses.

It is important to note that established publishers, academic or commercial, do not always meet their responsibility to bring important new knowledge to the public's attention. This is particularly the case when highly controversial materials are involved. In such instances, very small publishers are often willing to take the risk of publishing, or authors occasionally engage in self-publishing. A number of writers who later achieved great fame—such as James Joyce, Upton Sinclair, and Emma Goldman—were forced to publish their own books because no "reputable" firm was willing to issue them.[13] In countries where there is overt censorship by political, religious, or other authorities, the situation is, of course, very much more difficult.

Publishing is in part a sales enterprise. Most publishers pay considerable attention to the publicity and distribution of their books. Selling in the publishing world is often of a fairly genteel nature. Advertisements in appropriate newspapers and journals and direct mail campaigns are means of making information about books available. Specialized books are advertised in academic journals. Publishers try to have their books reviewed in appropriate media, believing that independent reviews help sell books. All of these efforts assume that the journals, mailing lists, book reviewers, book trade publications, and other media exist. Most industrialized nations are endowed with the basic book trade publicity mechanisms, but the situation in Third World nations is much less favorable.

A final yet quite important aspect in the distribution chain for books is the bookseller. While publishers have little direct control over book selling, their policies with regard to discounts, returns, and other factors directly affect the bookseller. Bookstores in many countries are inadequate in quality, and there are too few of them. In many countries, bookstores are located in metropolitan areas and in intellectual centers, with few elsewhere.[14] In a sense, the center-periphery situation discussed above with regard to nations also functions within countries, with large parts of most countries virtually cut off from exposure to current books on serious and scholarly topics.

Book publishing remains one element of communications in an increasingly diversified society which does not require large amounts of money. Successful long-term publishing does demand considerable capital and business enterprise, but it is possible to enter publishing on a small scale and have success. It has been estimated that it takes about $20,000 to produce a single scholarly title in the United States.[15] As a result of the economic reality of publishing, there are a large number of publishing firms in most industrialized nations, representing many diverse cultural, political, and other interests. Even in Third World nations, it is easier to start a publishing firm than a newspaper. Although it is relatively easy to start a publishing firm, it is more difficult to sustain an active publishing program, and even more difficult to earn a profit from publishing. This is particularly true for scholarly books, which have a limited sales potential and which are often difficult to market.

This summary of the role of the publisher by no means does justice to what is a complex undertaking. A publisher is a businessman, an intellectual, a publicity agent, a grammarian, and, hopefully in the long run, a teacher. The publisher is a gatekeeper who has considerable control over the kinds of knowledge that are available in a society.[16] The importance of publishing is perhaps exemplified in authoritarian societies, which make major efforts to control what is published and often destroy books considered subversive of public order or the approved ideology.

THE "CRISIS" OF PUBLISHING

In the first part of this chapter, a number of fairly constant variables affecting publishing have been discussed. These factors tend to affect publishers—and intellectual life generally—in a consistent, predictable manner. Literacy rates rise only slowly, and the basic purchasing power of a population rises or falls fairly slowly. However, publishing is currently faced with a series of unprecdicted crises which will affect its ability to serve the intellectual needs of most countries in the future. This section highlights some of those problems.

Perhaps the most serious problem affecting publishers is economic. The economic situation affects publishing in a number of ways. Basically, publishers are faced with a cost-price squeeze that threatens to price many kinds of books out of the market. This is particularly the case for scholarly books, which usually have a fairly high price because of small printings, and quality paperbacks, which find fewer buyers at high prices. University presses, which are financially marginal operations in the best of times, have been hit hardest by the inflationary spiral.

It is not difficult to understand the cause of the present situation. The cost of paper, for example, has doubled in the United States in one year. In some countries the increase has been even larger. Printing ink, labor, and even overhead have increased dramatically in cost. All this has meant that the prices of books go up and that capital expenditures rise significantly. Books are not a necessity for most people, and when economically pressed, individuals will decrease their purchases of books. The situation is perhaps even more serious in the Third World, where publishing is a marginal enterprise even in prosperous times.

At a time when publishers have been faced with inflationary pressures, the main purchasers of scholarly books—libraries and those connected with educational institutions—have been hit with the same crisis. In addition, universities in the United States and in a number of other countries have been faced with their own special crises—declining enrollments and political pressures, for example—and both academic libraries and faculty members have cut down on their purchases of books. Libraries find themselves able to purchase fewer books because individual volumes cost more. As sales drop for particular titles, printings tend to decline, and thus the retail price of a book rises even more precipitously than the rate of inflation. There is no question that the economic situation is a most serious matter for publishing. Inflation, the crisis in the universities, and severe shortages of materials—particularly paper—have combined to place publishers in an unprecedented crisis.

The proliferation of books has also created a problem. American publishers have claimed that there are "too many books."[17] Publishers in many countries experienced a considerable boom during the 1960s, when educational systems expanded rapidly and library budgets rose. This boom resulted in an increase in the number of titles published. However, the recent constriction of the market for books has made the wide variety of titles more difficult to sell. The competition for sales is very fierce, and in a market which is not growing dramatically, it is increasingly difficult for a publisher to function on an economically viable basis. There is insufficient space in bookstores for the number of new books published, libraries find it difficult to purchase and store the new publications, and readers cannot keep up with the flow. Part of the cause for this situation is the much-discussed knowledge explosion—the increase in research on many topics which inevitably led to the production of books, journal articles, and other means of reporting research findings.

Publishing has also seen a specialization of the market for books that has created a number of problems for the industry. This is perhaps especially the case for scholarly books. University presses in the United States print about as many copies of a single title today as they did fifteen or twenty years ago. The number of titles has increased dramatically, but the number of sales per title has not, despite the fact that the number of university faculty members has more than doubled. This phenomenon is due largely to the specialization which is endemic in academe—the facts that scholars tend to be experts on more and more narrow topics and that scholarly books are increasingly written for more limited audiences. It may be worth noting that the same thing has happened to general interest magazines in the United States. The demise of *Life* and *Look* and the growth of special interest magazines is indicative of a societal trend. Specialization means that the publisher has a small market for some kinds of books and that rising costs cannot be offset by larger editions.

A new technology that might make it possible to deal with some of these problems—inflated costs, knowledge explosion, and extreme specialization coupled with limited audiences—is in the process of development. Although industrialized nations are usually responsible for technological innovations, developing countries are indirectly affected by these changes. New methods of printing and composition, such as photo-offset, computer-based typography, and other innovations are beginning to change the economics of publishing. Publishers are only starting to use the technological innovations which are available. This is particularly true of scholarly publishers, who have been slow to innovate. Entirely new means of information presentation, such as the use of microfiche instead of books printed on paper, are other innovations which have potential implications for publishing. "Books" on microfiche can be "printed" on demand very cheaply once the original copy is made. Information can be stored in a very small area, thereby potentially revolutionizing the traditional library.

Developing countries are only now considering the implications of some of these innovations, and offset printing is coming into widespread use in the Third World. The point of these comments is that publishing, like other sectors of the economy, will necessarily have to deal with the impact of technology. Such consideration is at present in its very early stages. Change, however, is inevitable as economic factors price traditional books out of the market, as libraries cannot cope with the bulk of new books, and as new technological innovations are perfected.

The implications of photocopying, for example, have widespread relevance for publishing. Discussions of the meaning of copyright in the United States are heated in an era when individuals can make inexpensive photocopies of books and when libraries share materials through the photocopy process.[18] In Sweden, the principle of royalty payment for the use of books in libraries was recently established. Methods of providing payment to authors and publishers for the use of their materials or for photocopying books or articles are now under consideration in a number of countries. Many of the traditional notions concerning the production, distribution, and use of books are being called into question by technological innovations. Indeed, the very concept of the book as it has been known since the seventeenth century may be in the process of change.

This discussion of some of the aspects of the crisis of modern book publishing, and particularly the publishing of serious works of science, politics, and research, brings us back to our original theme. Publishers are part of an intellectual system which consists of both the circulation of ideas and trends in a society and economic and institutional structures. Publishers are affected not only by intellectual currents, but also by economic and other factors which have implications for the rest of society. Inflation, changes in technology, and other occurrences have direct implications for publishers. The industry is also affected by the institutional structures of society, the educational system, libraries, and copyright regulations.

Publishers are not powerless ciphers in their social milieu. They have considerable power over the kinds of materials which reach the mainstream of a society. They function as gatekeepers and arbiters of literary taste and culture. There is considerable interaction between editors and authors, and this interaction often shapes the nature of what is published. At the scholarly level, the kinds of books published have implications for the direction of research, for academic careers, and indirectly for currents of intellectual life. It is imperative, therefore, that both publishers and those involved in the intellectual enterprise understand the system which affects the publication of books. This system, often seemingly irrational, is in reality quite complex.

Chapter 2

Literary Colonialism: Books in the Third World

The products of knowledge are distributed unequally. Industrialized countries using a "world" language—notably, the United States, Britain, France, and, to a lesser extent, West Germany and the Soviet Union—are at the center of scientific research and scholarly productivity. As already noted, these same countries dominate the systems which distribute knowledge; they control publishing houses and produce scholarly journals, magazines, films, and television programs which the rest of the world consumes. Other countries, especially those in the Third World, are at the periphery of the international intellectual system.

This chapter will examine the relationship between industrialized and developing countries in the world of books and publishing. The discussion is predicated on several ideas. First, the unequal distribution of intellectual products results from a complex set of factors including historical events, economic relationships, language, literacy, and the nature of educational systems. Second, industrialized nations have benefited from their control of the means for distribution of knowledge and have at times used their superiority to the disadvantage of developing countries. Third, patterns of national development, the direction and rate of scientific growth, and the quality of cultural life are related to issues of intellectual productivity and independence. Third World nations have not often paid sufficient attention to these issues because of their overwhelming concern with more immediate problems of development.

There are not enough books to meet the rapidly growing needs of the developing countries. The shortage is not a problem which can be solved simply by printing vast quantities of books, but a complex issue which involves a number of national needs, from printing technology to research support. Some Third World countries lack the technical facilities for mass production of books, and some lack indigenous authors to write on subjects of national concern in languages that most literate citizens understand. Even where books exist to serve a national culture, they often cost more than individuals or even institutions can afford.

At present, there is a shortage of books for 70 percent of the globe.[1] The nature of the Third World "book hunger," as Barker and Escarpit have called it, can be seen in the fact that the 34 industrialized countries, with only 30 percent of the world's population, produce 81 percent of the world's book titles.[2] Although literacy rates in these nations are higher than in developing countries, the rates alone do not begin to account for the disparity in book production.

Figures for Asia dramatically illustrate the book gap. In 1967 the 18 developing countries of the region, with 28 percent of the world's population, accounted for only 7.3 percent of the total number of book titles and 2.6 percent of the total number of copies produced per year, and half of these were textbooks.[3] This represents only 32 book titles per million population, while in Europe the average was 417 per million. Since the late 1960s, when these statistics were collected, the volume of book output has increased, and in some areas, such as Southeast Asia, the situation has improved. But overall, the general configuration of inequality and shortage remains. It should be noted that, if anything, the situation for Africa has deteriorated.

Not only are too few books produced in developing countries, but the kinds of books published may not serve national priorities. For example, only 10 percent of all book titles published in India are concerned with pure and applied sciences. By comparison, 54 percent of the books published in the Soviet Union and 25 percent in the United States are on scientific subjects. While nations differ in the types of books they read, it is clear that India and other Third World nations need more scientific books than they are now publishing. As we shall see, many of the books used in the Third World are imported from the industrialized countries or are reprinted or translated volumes of Western origin, and such books may not be appropriate for developing countries' needs.

Book publishing does not function in a vacuum; as discussed in chapter 1, it is related to other elements in a society and has international dimensions as well. The following discussion will not analyze all elements of publishing in developing countries—a complex process in any society. Rather, it will treat those particular weaknesses of Third World publishing which perpetuate the dependent position in which most developing nations find themselves.

This is not to say that Third World publishing is totally dependent on industrial cultures or that accomplishments have not been achieved. Indeed, given the odds against creative independent publishing, a number of developing nations have made impressive gains. Nor should it be inferred that industrialized nations have manipulated Third World publishing solely for their own national interests and economic gain. Third World dependence on industrial nations for intellectual products results from a complex set of interrelated factors.

The colonial past remains a major influence on the intellectual and educational life of many developing areas and has had considerable impact on publishing as well. Traditional intellectual institutions atrophied under colonialism. Employment in the modern sector was linked to knowledge of the colonial language and to European education. Gradually, the colonial language became the medium for commerce, politics, science, and government.

Colonial languages have been used as a means of national unification in a number of Third World nations, particularly those in which no one indigenous language commands the loyalty of the entire population. In addition, ruling elites in Third World countries have often used the colonial language to protect their own privileged position. As long as only 10 percent or less of a population has access to the language of political and economic control, that language represents a source of power.

The colonial language has also been the medium for scholarship. The continued domination of the highest levels of the education system by Western languages has resulted in a paucity of technical and scholarly books in indigenous languages. English or French continues to be a key to graduate education and to research studies in the Third World, even in countries with some commitment to indigenous languages.

Furthermore, libraries and institutions, which comprise the bulk of the market for scholarly and nonfiction books, are accustomed to buying books in European languages. Even where classes are conducted in the indigenous language, a Western language is usually necessary for library research. Thus, authors wishing to write for a national audience and to reach their intellectual peers generally write in a European language.

Even in Indonesia, one of the few former colonies which has made a concentrated and fairly successful effort to promote the use of an indigenous language, Bahasa Indonesia, indigenous scholarly books and advanced textbooks do not yet exist and materials in English are widely used. It is my estimate that in India about half of the book titles are published in English, while only 2 percent of the population is literate in English. In both anglophone and francophone Africa, virtually all books are published in the metropolitan language. In many former colonies the 80 to 95 percent of the population who do not know English or French are effectively barred from the higher levels of education.[4]

Publishers are an integral part of this colonial tradition. Indian publishers, for example, do not follow a consciously neocolonialist policy of trying to maintain foreign influence on the subcontinent. Rather, they perceive that the largest market for books is in English and that, in fact, the only national market is for such material. Hence, a complex web of economic and intellectual relationships and traditions makes it difficult to stop publishing in European languages.

In most countries, the home for intellectual activity is the university. Even in the industrialized nations, intellectual journals probably would not survive were it not for the academic market of university libraries and individual scholars. In the West, scholarly books are often published by nonprofit university presses, and universities, especially those in the United States, emphasize research and publication as the main criteria for promotion and academic success. Faculty members are allowed time for research activities, and funding is often available.

In developing countries, research is not always a fundamental part of the academic enterprise and scholarly publication is not always seen as a key to professional advancement, largely because the nineteenth century British and French institutions—models for many Third World universities—did not emphasize research. In addition, many faculty members are too busy with heavy teaching loads, or with such external responsibilities as advising government agencies, to pursue research interests.

Conditions for research are often poor: funding is negligible; laboratories and computer facilities are rare; and while universities in developing countries are fairly well endowed by local standards, library facilities on the level of Western institutions are often lacking. Faculty salaries are seldom high enough to cover the price of books and journals, and, what is perhaps most important, colleagues and students provide little impetus for research within the university. Without the material resources and the academic subculture to stimulate research and writing, Third World universities contribute less than they might to the production of research and knowledge.

For those intellectuals outside the university structure, the situation is worse. While the economic rewards for intellectual work are not great in any country, they are particularly meager in the Third World. In general, intellectuals lack adequate working conditions and can obtain little public financial support for their work. Few journals and publishing houses exist to provide outlets for scholarly writing. Due to low literacy levels in developing nations, there is only a small audience for either scholarly or nonscholarly work. With neither public support nor a large book-buying public, very few intellectuals can support themselves solely on the basis of their writing or research.[5]

Therefore, Third World intellectuals tend to look toward a Western audience. If there is prestige in publishing, it lies in writing for such Western journals as *Encounter* or *Les Temps Modernes,* or in having a book published in London, New York, or Paris. Publication abroad may bring money and the opportunity to communicate with other Third World intellectuals, since communication seldom runs directly between one developing country and another but is mediated through advanced nations.

There is little circulation of books or journals among Third World nations, even between those with the same language. It is significant that *Jeune Afrique,* an influential African journal with a multinational circulation, is published in Paris. The enterprising Nigerian publisher Joseph Okpaku came to New York to start his Third Press, which specializes in African and black subjects. It is perhaps indicative of the difficulties involved in regional publishing that it is often easier to travel between Dakar or Abidjan and Paris than between various African capitals.

The economics of publishing concerns much more than the cost of producing a book in a particular country. Rates of literacy, reading habits of the population, government policy toward books, copyright regulations, and the nature of libraries are all part of the economic equation.[6] For example, low literacy rates, low per capita purchasing power, and a diversity of languages—all common in Third World nations—contribute to a limited market for books. Many of the smaller developing countries find it economically impossible to publish most kinds of books because the internal market is simply too small. Even in such large nations as Nigeria, India, and Indonesia, only some textbooks, certain kinds of popular fiction, and religious books are profitable to publish. Although labor costs are lower than in the West, total costs are high since print runs are small and distribution is difficult.

Book distribution may be the single most serious dilemma of publishing in the Third World. Dan Lacy divides the problem into three elements: (a) the actual demand for books as distinguished from the need; (b) the network of distribution, for example, booksellers and wholesalers; and (c) the means of conveying information about books, such as reviews, advertising, and book-trade journals. Low reader density, great distances between settlements, and poor transportation facilities make book distribution in developing countries particularly difficult.[7] Just as developing countries themselves are at the periphery of the world's knowledge system, regions outside of capital cities, especially rural areas, which are often completely without access to books, periodicals, or newspapers, are at the periphery of knowledge systems within these nations.[8]

An important part of the Third World's cultural dependency stems from political and trade relationships with industrialized nations. Industrialized nations export their products, in this case, books and expertise, to the developing countries. Foreign aid programs, while seeking to provide help to developing countries, often deepen existing patterns of dependence.[9] Knowledge, then, is a part of the neocolonial relationship.

Commercial arrangements built up over years of colonialism persist in many developing countries. Branches of British and French publishers continue to operate in the Third World, and in some places dominate the publishing scene.[10] The advantages of foreign firms—expertise, the backing of foreign capital, and a worldwide distribution network—have made the emergence of indigenous publishers even more difficult than might otherwise have been the case.

In general, French and British firms have dealt in commercially successful and uncontroversial textbooks, which constitute the overwhelming proportion of the book market in most Third World countries. These firms have published few original works by local authors, and many of their products are printed in Britain or France. In recent years, American publishers have followed the same pattern, establishing themselves in developing areas particularly where United States foreign aid programs have been active. The balance, however, is not entirely negative. Foreign firms provided an early base for publishing and increasingly have taken responsibility for training indigenous individuals as workers in the industry.

Foreign aid programs have had an impact on publishing in developing countries. While the United States has sponsored the largest aid effort, other countries have also engaged in aid programs. For example, the English Language Book Scheme (ELBS), sponsored by Britain, each year sells more than 1 million copies comprising several hundred titles intended mainly for use as college and university textbooks. On a smaller scale, France and the Federal Republic of Germany have active book programs, with France being particularly active in ensuring that its books are circulated in the francophone world. The Soviet Union has also been active. For example, in 1982 the Soviet Union produced 74.5 million books in 56 non-Soviet languages, all destined for export. The Soviets produced 11 million books in Spanish, making the USSR the sixth largest publisher of books in that language.[11]

Foreign aid, particularly intellectual assistance, cannot be separated from the policy goals of the donor country or, for that matter, from the policies and orientation of the recipient nation's government. The American rationale for book-related aid programs has involved both the technical importance of books in the development process and the ideological elements of anticommunism.[12] Between 1950 and 1964, the United States Information Agency assisted in the production of 9,000 editions and printed 80 million copies in 51 languages.[13]

In the aftermath of the Vietnam War in the 1970s, book programs assisted by the American government declined dramatically because education and culture were not emphasized in foreign-aid efforts. In the 1980s, however, the U.S. government has taken a renewed interest in books and culture as instruments of foreign assistance.

The Indo-American Textbook Program (PL480) was one of the largest American efforts. Under the PL480 program more than 1,000 different textbooks were reprinted in English for use by Indian college and university students, and more than 4 million copies were distributed at subsidized prices. Although the titles were predominantly in the natural sciences, the reprints included many topics in the social sciences and humanities. The Indian government gave full approval to the program, and a joint Indo-American committee selected the textbooks. With the cooling in Indo-American relations and changing U.S. foreign aid priorities, textbook aid has virtually ended in India.

Like similar programs in other countries, the Indo-American Textbook Program had certain negative results. In some fields, particularly the social sciences, American books were not relevant to the Indian situation, and the orientations of American social scientists reflected their own ideological biases. Yet the subsidized books tended to drive their more expensive unsubsidized domestic counterparts off the market. The artificially low prices for American books gave buyers a distorted sense of the real cost of books. Finally, several subsidiaries of U.S. publishers were able to establish themselves in the Indian market through the aid programs, and their growth may have retarded the development of indigenous Indian publishing.

Yet not all aspects of foreign book programs are pernicious. Aid programs place inexpensive books in the hands of students and can make textbooks in a range of disciplines quickly available. Such programs often provide technical assistance, printing, or other equipment to local publishers and sponsor translations into indigenous languages. It is necessary, however, to evaluate such programs carefully. Do aid programs help Third World publishers to establish strong roots and to bring out relevant locally written books? Or do they circulate materials which the industrialized countries think will win them influence at the cost of discouraging the development of local publishing? The answers to such questions are complicated, but certainly require more attention at the planning and implementation stages of aid programs than they have been given to date.

Another aspect of intellectual neocolonialism is the impact of Western research on the developing countries. Most research, particularly in technology and the natural sciences, is done in the West. Despite some efforts at research in the Third World, it is likely that this monopoly will persist—if anything, the developing countries will lag farther and farther behind. It is not that scholars in the Third World do not have the ability to do research; in India, such individuals as M. N. Srinivas and André Bétille in sociology have done outstanding work.

But, as noted earlier, the universities do not stress research, and funds are seldom available to finance it.

In fact, Western scholars have done much of the research on the Third World, and indigenous scholars often must learn about their own political system or agricultural situation through the writings of their Western counterparts. Certainly much of the Western scholarship has been useful and reasonably accurate; but as long as knowledge about the nature of society in developing countries is mediated through Western sources, it is suspect because of all the possible methodological and ideological biases, misperceptions and other problems such mediation may entail.[14] In addition, much scholarship and interpretation concerning the Third World is published in the West and is accessible only with difficulty in the developing countries themselves.

A final problem which developing countries face in their quest for intellectual independence is that of copyright, which traditionally has worked to the advantage of the industrialized nations and only now is beginning to change.[15] Copyright regulations have made it difficult and expensive for Third World nations to translate and publish materials originally appearing in the West. Western publishers have often preferred to export their own books rather than to license reprinting in developing nations because larger profits could be realized. Recently, changes in international copyright arrangements have permitted developing countries to reprint and/or translate educational materials more freely than before and at a modest cost.[16] These changes, made when the industrialized nations began to realize that copyright agreements were being violated with increasing frequency, have helped the developing countries obtain the printed materials they need at prices they can afford.

In a situation of considerably inequality, there is a limited amount that the Third World can do to establish independence immediately. Yet there are a number of strategies Third World nations can use to increase the independence of their intellectual life generally and of their publishing in particular.

A few Third World nations have attempted radical solutions to the problem of dependency, and the results have not been satisfactory. The best-known example, China, stressed an ideology of self-sufficiency in an attempt to redirect the educational system and intellectual life toward a completely indigenous orientation. These efforts were strengthened by severing many intellectual and cultural ties with the industrialized nations, by forcing intellectuals to become involved with the day-to-day problems of the peasantry through work in villages, and by stressing practical technology in schools and colleges. These policies, which reached their apogee during the Cultural Revolution, proved to be completely unsuccessful and resulted mainly in China's falling further behind in industrial and technological development. The current period has seen a complete reversal. China now stresses contact and close technological links with the industrialized nations. Having tried isolation, the Chinese authorities saw that the policy failed.[17]

Other Third World nations have used more modest means to achieve some degree of intellectual independence and indigenous cultural development. Some countries have stressed the use of a national language as a means of cultural unification. Others have severely limited the importation of Western films and, in some cases, books, in order to stress indigenous values. A few countries have allocated funds to projects, such as the National Book Trust in India, which promote local authorship, cultural development, and publishing. Finally, many Third World countries have nationalized textbook publishing to ensure that these books reflect values and orientations appropriate for national development. But with few exceptions, these efforts have been piecemeal. There has been little cooperation among Third World nations in joint cultural programs or even in sharing information and publications.

The following suggestions are intended to provide some ideas which can be easily implemented and which may help to ameliorate the existing inequalities in the world of books and publishing. These suggestions are realistic in the sense that no major changes in the relationships between industrialized and Third World nations are required to implement them. Clearly, more radical solutions to the problems of inequality are needed to effect basic change. But to suggest modest reforms is not to deny the need to radically restructure the relationship between the rich and poor nations.

As a first step, communications between Third World nations should be improved so that common problems and issues can be discussed directly without being mediated through institutions and publications in the industrialized nations. This is particularly important on a regional basis, for example, among the nations of francophone Africa and of Southeast Asia. As a part of communications development, Third World countries must also create viable means of book distribution among themselves, and between themselves and the industrialized nations.

With the strengthening of indigenous publishing and internal distribution facilities in the Third World, intellectuals need not publish their work abroad. Such an effort should include financial and technical assistance from the public sector when necessary. Foreign scholars working in developing nations should publish their findings in the countries where they conduct their research. In this way local publishing will be strengthened and relevant research will be available to local audiences. The intellectual infrastructure in many Third World countries needs to be strengthened in other ways. Libraries, journals which review books, and bibliographical and publicity tools for publishing should be supported.

In addition, major national policy questions which relate directly to books, including the language of instruction in the educational system, levels of literacy, and the ownership of the publishing apparatus, must be solved by Third World governments with an understanding of their implications for the balance of intellectual production. Part of any language reform effort should be assistance to publishing in indigenous languages. Finally, Third World leaders must carefully evaluate foreign aid programs to ensure that their nations benefit without local publishing industries or intellectual autonomy being undermined.

These are but a few suggestions for the solution of a complex problem. While publishing is a small part of the relationship between industrialized and developing countries, Third World nations can institute reforms in the publishing process because massive financial investments are not required and power politics are not involved. Through understanding the complexities of the issue, individuals in both industrialized and developing countries may be able to begin exploring constructive solutions.

Chapter 3

Scholarly Publishing in the Third World

The creation and dissemination of knowledge is a complex process in any society, and is particularly difficult in the Third World, where the economic, intellectual, and institutional structures of the scientific community are not well established. This chapter focuses on the dissemination of knowledge in the Third World.[1] It is predicated on the idea that knowledge dissemination is especially important in the Third World context, since the emergence of an independent intellectual life and some self-sufficiency in the scientific realm depend in part on building the structures for knowledge dissemination. This discussion begins with the special problems facing the Third World in terms of scholarly publishing and then discusses the possible roles of the university press in this context. Given the paucity of data on this topic, the discussion is necessarily somewhat general and is aimed both at analyzing some current problems and at stimulating thought concerning one creative means of fulfilling an urgent building block in the structure of intellectual development.

This chapter focuses largely on universities in the process of creation and dissemination of knowledge, and special attention is paid to the university press as a means of communication. While universities do not have a monopoly on either creation or distribution of knowledge, they are, especially in the Third World, the key institutions in this process. They house the large share of creative scholars, sponsor most functioning research institutes, provide stimulation for scholarly life through the norms of academic life, and in the Third World are often the center of the intellectual life of the nation. This has not always been the case; up to a century ago many scientific discoveries were made by independent intellectuals, and at present, work in the applied sciences in some countries is often done in industrial or government-sponsored laboratories. While universities play a key role in knowledge distribution in the English-speaking countries, some European nations rely on books and journals issued by private publishers for much of their scholarly publishing. Despite these exceptions, universities stand at the center of the scientific and intellectual process in many nations, especially those of the Third World, and therefore deserve considerable attention.

This discussion is based on several simple but not widely discussed ideas regarding the Third World. The need for Third World countries to establish independence in all spheres of modern life, including intellectual life, is critically important, and publishing is one small way to build such independence. As one observer put it, "To establish an indigenous publishing house is an act of liberation, and therefore a necessity, because it breaks the control, indeed the monopoly which the white races have over the world literature, for which reason they have controlled the mind of the African."[2] The intellectual "system" of which publishing is a part is complicated and requires a considerable infrastructure (see chapter 1). It is not enough for an author to write a manuscript. There must be technical means of transforming that manuscript into a book, the editorial expertise to coordinate the process, the means of distribution and promotion, and a readership interested in reading the products of research and intellectual work. While publishing is relatively inexpensive in terms of investment of capital and equipment, it requires coordination of such elements as educational institutions, printers, authors, editors, booksellers, journals, and others.[3]

SPECIAL THIRD WORLD PROBLEMS

Publishing, as well as other elements of an industrialized society, faces special problems in the Third World. The infrastructures which are so important to publishing are often missing. In particularly short supply are skilled editors, designers, distribution experts, and others who are necessary in the book production process. While printing equipment and paper supplies are often available, they are in many cases imported and therefore expensive. Modern publishing is very much part of a network of communications within a society, and it is very difficult to establish one element of the network without the entire circle of communications.

Books need to be publicized and distributed. Scholarly books are particularly difficult to distribute adequately since the market is small and dispersed over a wide geographical area. In the Third World, distribution is especially difficult because of transportation problems, an especially small market, few channels for publicizing books, limited bibliographical tools, and the general level of poverty.[4]

Literacy rates in the Third World tend to be low—from 40 percent in India, more than 50 percent in many Latin American nations, to as little as 10 percent in some African nations. Perhaps more relevant to a consideration of scholarly publishing is the fact that the number of academics tend to be small and enrollments in higher education limited. General purchasing power is very limited, with per capita annual incomes of $300 or less in many nations, and it is impossible for the large majority of the population to buy books. In many Third World nations, even academics, who rank near the top of the income scale, find it difficult to afford to purchase books and journals. A network of libraries—which in industrialized nations account for up to 80 percent of the total purchases of scholarly books—is generally lacking in the Third World, thereby denying the publishing industry a key market. It is estimated that in India, libraries account for between 80 percent and 90 percent of purchases of scholarly books. India, with its 3,500 colleges and 120 universities, provides a fairly substantial institutional market for books. Most other Third World nations have fewer libraries and similar institutions.

Many Third World nations are faced with language problems which impinge directly on book publishing. The legacy of colonialism has left many Asian and African nations with educational systems which function largely in a foreign language—English or French—which is understood by only a small fraction of the indigenous population. The lack of a common indigenous language in many Third World countries, the wishes of an entrenched elite, and the inherent difficulties of shifting communications media for education, government, and the economy are among the problems which have led to the continuing influence of European languages throughout the Third World.[5] The language problem is a serious one for the Third World in many respects, and it has major implications for publishing as well. For example, as has already been mentioned, close to one-half of the books published in India annually are in English, yet only 2 percent of the Indian population is literate in English. Efforts to develop Swahili in East Africa have been hindered by the lack of a publishing apparatus, reluctance of some Africans to use the language, and other factors. Indonesia has been more successful in establishing one of its languages as the national language and the key medium for book publishing. Policymakers and scholars are faced with the dilemma of whether to publish in a European language and thereby broaden the market for their books, or to use an indigenous medium and immediately truncate the market—and probably the impact—of their books.

Third World nations are in many respects still dependent on the industrialized countries. One of these dependencies is in the area of knowledge creation and distribution. The major universities, research institutes, libraries, journals, and publishing firms are located in the industrialized nations. The bulk of the funds spent for scientific research is spent in the West. The major languages of intellectual discourse and of scientific research are Western languages, predominantly English and French. In much of anglophone Africa, for example, publishing is dominated by firms based in the industrialized nations, especially Britain.[6] These firms publish most of the scholarly books, as well as a large share of the textbooks of those countries, and because of their entrenched position, make the emergence of indigenous publishers difficult. Third World nations are, in a sense, at the periphery of the world system of knowledge, with the industrialized nations at the center of that system.[7] This situation, which some analysts have called "dependency," is in part a natural result of the legacy of colonialism, the imbalance in the world's scientific production, and the general internal problems of the Third World—poverty, illiteracy, the lack of a large educational system, and many others.

Another element which contributes to the continued intellectual domination of Western countries over the Third World is the deliberate policies of the industrialized nations to maintain their power. These policies have been called "neocolonialism," and they operate in the arena of education and intellectual life, as well as in other areas.[8] Neocolonialism is maintained through foreign aid programs, loan policies of the industrialized nations, and in other ways. While a detailed analysis of neocolonialism is beyond the scope of this essay, it is a factor which must be considered in any analysis of publishing in the Third World.

SCHOLARLY PUBLISHING: THE CURRENT SITUATION

Given the seemingly insurmountable problems mentioned above, it is surprising that any scholarly publishing takes place in the Third World. Yet, scholarly books—those publications which report research findings, comment on academic matters, or in general are aimed at an audience of intellectuals—do get published. This section discusses some of the problems of scholarly publishing and surveys the current situation in some Third World nations.

In part due to the work of international agencies like UNESCO, Third World governments have at least given some attention to the development of a book industry and the production of books. Most Third World nations have built up at minimum a rudimentary publishing industry, and are now able to issue school textbooks, literacy materials, and similar educational book materials.

There has been relatively little recognition at the governmental level of the importance of scholarly publishing. Universities have not taken much interest in fostering scholarly publishing, and when they have been involved in the publishing enterprise at all, it has with a few exceptions been at the level of providing textbooks for their own students, often in fields where indigenously produced texts did not exist. The concern for educational publishing in the Third World has for the most part been aimed at the production of textbooks and other curricular materials for all levels of the educational system, and for nonformal educational programs such as literacy efforts. Among the most successful government-sponsored publishing efforts in the Third World are the Casa de Libros in Cuba, the Dewan Bahasa dan Pustaka in Malaysia, and the National Book Trust in India, all of which have been concerned with the production of basic literacy materials, textbooks, and to some extent with sponsoring books on cultural and intellectual topics.

It is not surprising that official concern with publishing has been for the very practical—and usually elementary—book needs of developing Third World economies. Scholarly books are considered to be less urgent than provision of textbooks where none at present exist. Even at the university level, scholars have been concerned with writing textbooks for undergraduate courses or simply with translating Western textbooks into indigenous languages because of a lack of such books. The minority of Third World universities with printing and publishing facilities has generally used these facilities for the immediate printing needs of their institutions—usually examination forms and textbooks—rather than for scholarly publishing.

While clear statistics are unavailable, it is possible to estimate that the bulk of scholarly books in the Third World come from two main sources at the present time. These two sources are (1) publishers in the industrialized countries, who export their books to the Third World; and (2) commercial and, occasionally, governmental publishers in the Third World. Universities have only recently entered publishing, although in a few cases they are actively participating in scholarly publishing programs. It is likely that the majority of scholarly books still originate outside the Third World and are published in Western languages.

The foreign origin of many scholarly books has several implications. Most are written by Western scholars and scientists. Good scholarship is in many ways culture-free, but the ideological orientations of Western scholars, the nature of their training, and the kinds of interests which are engendered by Western academic culture certainly have an impact on scholarship. Furthermore, the research questions which may be relevant to Western scientists may not be especially useful to the Third World. Books published in the industrialized nations are in many cases more expensive than domestically published works, and their distribution in most Third World nations tends to be slow and difficult. Imported books are a small drain on the foreign exchange reserves of the Third World as well, and international copyright regulations and patterns of book distribution generally work against the Third World.[9] Perhaps most important, books published in the industrialized nations are written, edited, and published for an audience in these countries and not to meet the needs of the Third World.

At the present time, most scholarly books published in the Third World are issued by private commercial publishers, except, of course, in those countries which do not have private publishers. In most of Africa and in parts of Southeast Asia, the majority of such indigenous scholarly publishing is carried out by local branches of foreign publishing firms such as Oxford University Press and Macmillan. This situation is a remnant of colonialism and has had a major impact on indigenous publishing.[10] Most of these "expatriate" publishers are from the former colonial power, although in recent years American firms have been increasingly active in Third World nations.

With the exception of a few university presses, the publication of scholarly books, research monographs, and the like is very much a sideline for indigenous Third World publishers. Scholarly publishing is not viable commercially as a mainstay of a profit-making business, although publishers in some countries indicate that scholarly books do break even or make a small profit, but only after a long period of time. Editions tend to be small—1,000 seems to be an average printing, with 800 not unusual.[11] Private-sector publishers find their main profit in textbooks and sometimes in general book publishing, and scholarly books are a sideline done as a public service or to maintain prestige in the academic community, often the major customer for textbooks.

Distribution of scholarly books is a problem in any nation, and it is particularly difficult in the Third World. The national book markets, even in nations as large as India or Indonesia, are small due to the lack of purchasing power of individual academics, the limited number of libraries, and similar factors. Book exports to other Third World nations are a problem which has not been solved. Networks of publicity and commerce tend to run between England, France, and more recently the United States and the former colony. It has been said that it is easier in the Ivory Coast to obtain a book published in Paris than a book from neighboring Senegal. Publishers, distributors, and the intellectual public tend to look to the major Western centers for most intellectual needs, and the products of other Third World nations are not considered prestigious. Thus, intellectual tradition has combined with commercial patterns to make trade among Third World nations difficult. There have been few efforts to bridge this gap, perhaps in part because Third World publishers have turned to the relatively lucrative and easily reached academic markets in the United States and Britain as an outlet for their scholarly books.

As noted earlier, the lack of the usual infrastructures for book distribution constitutes a severe problem for the dissemination of scholarly books in the Third World. It is often easier for a Nigerian librarian to find out what books have been published on a given topic in Britain or the United States than it is to locate relevant titles published in the Ivory Coast, India, or Tanzania. This is simply because there are well-developed bibliographical resources in the industrialized nations, but few such resources in the Third World. Similarly, the major media for scholarly book reviewing, the academic journals, are for the most part published in the West, and these seldom review books published in the Third World. Local journals are few in number and seldom read beyond their nation of publication.

The term *Third World* has been used in this chapter as if it were possible to generalize broadly about a range of nations which share little except a low per capita income and a common desire to industrialize. There are many differences among Third World nations with regard to scholarly publishing, as well as in most other spheres. Third World nations range from India, which has a large and active publishing industry and which issues a large number of scholarly books each year, to small nations such as Swaziland or Burundi, which have virtually no possibility of creating a viable publishing industry of any kind due to economic realities and a tiny potential reading public.

Several Latin American nations, notably Mexico, Brazil, and Argentina, have well-developed publishing industries and manage to issue a substantial number of scholarly books. Latin America constitutes a continental market for scholarly books, and this situation has helped to stimulate publishing. Such regional markets in other parts of the Third World are only now emerging. Efforts are being made in anglophone and francophone Africa, where the continued use of European languages for scholarly purposes is unquestioned. The situation in Asia is more complex due to the existence of several dominant nations which have so far not attempted to establish regional markets for their books. India is the largest publishing country in the region, and has made some efforts to promote its books. Indonesia has as yet only a small book industry, and its commitment to the use of Bahasa Indonesia as the language of education and publishing limits its access to foreign markets. China has thus far not played an active role in scholarly book publishing in the area. At present, only Latin America has a functioning regional market for scholarly books, and other regions are hampered by the lack of such arrangements for book distribution.

It is fair to say that with the possible exception of India, Mexico, and Argentina, the scholarly publishing needs of the Third World are not being adequately met, regardless of the language of publishing or even of the origin of relevant books. Commercial publishers simply cannot expend the resources necessary to publish scholarly books, and no agencies have emerged in most countries to fill the gap. It is in this context that a consideration of the present role and future possibilities of the university press is relevant.[12]

THE UNIVERSITY PRESS: ITS ROLE AND POSSIBILITIES

The university press is not the only means of scholarly publishing. Indeed, it has strength mainly in the English-speaking nations of the United States, Canada, and Britain, with toeholds in Japan and a few other industrialized countries. The bulk of the world's scholarly output is no doubt issued by publishers other than universities. Even in the United States, specialized private scholarly publishers have recently found it possible to make a modest profit on academic books and journals, while the university presses have had to cut back because of economic stringency and still operate for the most part at a loss.[13] It should also be recognized that government subsidies to academic libraries in the United States were a key factor in maintaining the profitability of scholarly publishing—even in the nation with the largest university system, scholarly publishing could not take place without indirect subsidy. In the Third World, university publishing is in its infancy and libraries are not as well developed or as numerous. The reason that the university press is considered at some length in this chapter is that it offers a unique model for scholarly publishing in the Third World.

Scholarly publishing almost inevitably is an unprofitable undertaking and often requires a direct or indirect subsidy. As one expert noted concerning university presses, "We publish the smallest editions at the greatest cost, and on these we place the highest price, and then we try to market them to people who can least afford them."[14] In the context of the Third World, subsidies are virtually mandatory, and the university press offers a means of accepting outside subsidy—almost inevitably from government sources—and still maintaining independence of judgment and autonomous decision making. It is almost axiomatic that creative and independent publishing must have a great deal of autonomous judgment. Publishing at its best is a professional activity, and external interference in the direct decisions of a publishing firm can only lower standards. Publishers must, however, be accountable—not only to the scholarly public which will purchase their books, but also to some extent to those who provide subsidies.

While university publishing has a long history—extending from the origins of Oxford University Press in 1478—it has come into its own in the past century, particularly in the United States, where at least fifty university presses now operate. University presses are well established in relatively few nations. While university presses also exist to a very limited extent in other European countries, they play a small role in publishing in those countries. In much of Europe, scholarly publishing is accomplished by private firms. This is the pattern in the German-speaking countries, in France, and in Holland. In the socialist countries of Eastern Europe, scholarly publishing is carried out both by some general publishing houses (which are, of course, state-owned) and by the publishing arms of various scientific institutes and agencies. The Eastern European model, which is also followed to some extent in other parts of the world (in the United States, for example, the Smithsonian Institution and some other large scientific agencies have their own publishing divisions), may also provide a useful model for the Third World.

In its American manifestation, the university press has as its basic role to publish scholarly books and to distribute them to the relevant audience. Scholarly books are defined broadly to include research monographs, analyses of current problems from a scholarly viewpoint, literary criticism, and the like. In a sense, the university presses try to publish materials of high quality which are not destined for commercial success (although as direct and indirect subsidies for academic presses have become more limited in recent years, the scholarly publishers have taken commercial viability increasingly into account). The average press run of a university press book is fairly low—1,500 is a common figure—and most scholarly books take three or more years to sell out. University press publications tend to be expensive, in part because of limited printings, and in part because of high-quality production standards and frequently complicated typography.

The American university press emerged at a time when American higher education was declaring its independence from European models and was beginning to emphasize graduate study and research. In a sense, the university press was part of America's effort to declare intellectual independence in the late nineteenth century. It permitted scholarly publishing to develop in the United States at a time when there was little likelihood that private publishers would take on this responsibility. It is not surprising that the early presses emerged at such institutions as Johns Hopkins, Chicago, and Cornell—all universities which made a firm commitment to graduate education at the end of the nineteenth century. The "golden age" of the American university press might be considered to be the 1960s and early 1970s, when unprecedented federal funds were available for library purchases and institutions were expanding at a rapid rate. The dissemination of knowledge was a part of this process of growth. The university presses were a useful means of funneling foundation grants and other funds into publishing while still maintaining considerable independence over the publishing operation.

In many respects, the universities of the Third World find themselves in a situation not unlike that of the United States at the turn of the last century. Many Third World universities are moving quickly toward an emphasis on graduate training and research after a long period in which such activities were not emphasized. There is a growing realization that the production of indigenous scientific research and analysis is important. In the social sciences and humanities, indigenous scholarship has been especially emphasized. While links to an international scientific community are still strong, efforts are under way to provide an independent base for research and scholarship. The pressures on Third World universities are immense—to provide undergraduate education to a rapidly growing middle class, to develop graduate programs, to contribute directly to the processes of modernization, and to foster scientific research. Despite these pressures, some universities are moving toward an active research and scientific environment, from which scholarly publications have begun to emerge.

At the present time, university presses in the Third World are in an early stage of development. A minority of nations has strong university presses, although few if any are in the Western mold completely. Most university presses have as their major task the production of textbooks and related materials for use in higher education. Scholarly publishing is at best an ancillary activity. Even the branches of Oxford University Press engage in much nonscholarly publishing in the Third World. Given the multiple needs of Third World universities, it is likely that university publishing in the "pure" sense of the term is probably impossible, and there will inevitably be a linking of practical services to the educational community with the more narrow but highly important role as a publisher of scholarly books. In most countries, university presses need to take their scholarly roles more seriously, but some kind of balance must be maintained.

The Indian situation will provide an indication of the role of the university press. With approximately 120 universities and 3 million students in post-secondary education, there are perhaps 20 active university presses. The oldest, the University of Calcutta Press, was founded in 1908 and has published more than 1,000 titles. Ninety-one institutions of higher education in India indicate that they have some publishing programs, but most of these are inactive or have no relevance to scholarly publishing. The most active university presses issue a small number of scholarly books each year, and confine the bulk of their publishing efforts to the immediate printing needs of their university and to textbooks for classes in the university. There is virtually no cooperation among the university presses, and even the textbooks which are printed for one institution are not generally distributed beyond that institution. The small output of scholarly books is not distributed adequately—distribution efforts are in almost all cases significantly less adequate than those of the private-sector publishers. The quality of production is also generally lower than that of private publishers, although prices of university press books tend to be somewhat below those of the commercial house publications. In a few instances, university presses have turned their scholarly books over to private publishers for distribution, but these arrangements have usually not worked out very well.

Most Indian university presses are governed by academic boards composed of administrators and faculty members at the sponsoring institutions. This situation has to some extent insulated them from direct interference in their operations, although the pervasive academic politics evident in India has naturally affected the presses as well. Few university presses publish books by faculty members from outside their sponsoring institutions, and virtually none has attempted to build for itself a reputation of excellence in scholarly publishing. The scrutiny given to individual manuscripts which are submitted is limited, and most academic presses have little or no qualified editorial staff to ensure high standards of editing or production. In general, support for the presses is limited, and it is not unusual for them to earn a small profit for the university or at least save money by printing examination forms and other academic documents. The university presses, in short, have not developed an ethos or a mode of operation which will encourage excellence in scholarly publishing.

A large number of scientific institutions and government agencies also engage in publishing in India, but in general their efforts are not effective in that their books are not adequately distributed and standards of quality are often low. India, unlike most other Third World nations, has a sufficiently well-developed private publishing enterprise, so that the lack of a scholarly publishing apparatus in the universities is not very damaging to the publication of academic and scientific works. It is clear, however, that the nation would be served much better if current efforts by universities and other nonprofit agencies to publish their materials were better handled. In the long run, given the expansion of knowledge and the inherent difficulties of profitably publishing academic work, the emergence of an effective university press network in India is highly advisable.

Other Third World countries are, in general, less well served in terms of scholarly publishing than is India. Most of the scholarly books concerning a country as large as Nigeria are published outside the country or by expatriate firms within Nigeria. The establishment of university presses at two of Nigeria's leading universities during the past decade or so has improved that situation somewhat, but the output of books of most of these presses is very limited—perhaps ten to twenty new titles per year. The university presses are concerned with scholarly publishing, and have the potential of serving an important need, but the universities have not provided their presses with the necessary resources.[15] The situation in Ghana is similar, with the establishment of at least one university press in recent years and the emergence of a government-sponsored publishing house which has taken some interest in scholarly publishing.[16] Francophone African nations are poorly served by indigenous publishers of any sort, and the majority of the very small number of scholarly books published about these countries is generally published in France and exported back to Africa. Anglophone East Africa has seen the development of several private publishers, sometimes with the assistance of British firms, which have a strong interest in scholarly publishing.

Southeast Asia has seen perhaps the most active development of university presses, with especially strong interest in Malaysia, Singapore, and Hong Kong, where the influence of the British academic model and of Oxford University Press has been strong. The foundation of university presses in two of Malaysia's universities and the commitment of these presses to scholarly publishing have given academic publishing an energetic start. The University of Singapore Press also has a substantial list of scholarly books. In Hong Kong, the English-medium University of Hong Kong has a small but quite active university press, and the new Chinese University has entered the field of publishing as well. Other Asian nations, such as Taiwan, South Korea, and Indonesia, have expressed sporadic interest in university press publishing, and several presses have been established.

Few Latin American universities have scholarly presses as part of their operation, although the University of Buenos Aires Press has been, until the recent political difficulties in Argentina, actively engaged in scholarly publishing of a high standard. Several Mexican universities, including the Autonomous University and the Collegio de Mexico in Mexico City, have established scholarly presses. In most of the region, however, the limited amount of scholarly publishing that occurs is done by private firms.

It is clear that there is a need for more scholarly books in the Third World, as such books constitute one of the underpinnings of an independent intellectual and scientific life. It is also clear that in most Third World nations there is at present an inadequate supply of scholarly books, and that the means required to permit the publication of such books are lacking. There is a growing recognition that research and scholarly publication play an important part in nation building and development, but there is as yet only a limited understanding of how to foster the necessary publishing apparatus. All of this is at the theoretical level. There is less consensus about whether present conditions in the Third World can absorb more scholarly books—that is, whether the amount of scholarship now taking place and the size of the academic and intellectual communities can organizationally and financially support a scholarly publishing enterprise. As Ronald Barker and Robert Escarpit point out in their analysis of books in the Third World, there is often a difference between the objective need for books and the ability of a nation to produce and consume such books.[17] However, given the importance of publishing scholarly materials, it is probably better to have a temporary "surplus" of published knowledge than to let market forces take their course.

The dissemination of knowledge in the Third World is a complicated matter. Even at the level of relatively advanced research materials, the issue is multifaceted and relates to such matters as literacy rates, communications networks, the infrastructure of the printing and publishing industries, government policies, the orientation of universities, and other matters. While scholarly publishing is clearly not the key that will unlock the process of modernization and development, it is a small part of a total effort to build independent societies in the Third World. The whole process of the creation of an independent intellectual and scientific life has received very little attention in the literature, and the purpose of this chapter has been to highlight the role of one small element in that process—scholarly publishing—and to indicate how some of the seemingly insurmountable problems associated with it can be handled. Fortunately, the creation of an adequate means of scientific and academic communications in a nation through books and journals is neither very costly nor overwhelmingly difficult. Furthermore, it is a process which is a natural part of the academic enterprise. As universities grow in size and excellence, they will naturally turn to problems not only of creating new knowledge but of communicating this knowledge to the relevant publics.

Chapter 4

Center and Periphery: The Case of India

India serves as a particularly appropriate case study for a consideration of knowledge production and distribution. It shares with many Third World nations problems of poverty; low levels of literacy (approximately 40 percent); problems of political unrest; the pulls of ethnic, linguistic, and religious groups; and major issues of national integration. Further, India shares a colonial past with many other Third World nations. The continuing impact of the English language and of British educational and cultural policies affects contemporary India.

Yet, India is also a major producer and distributor of knowledge in its own right. India boasts the world's third-largest scientific community, and while the quality of many of these scientists and of some scientific institutions is deficient, there is a scientific infrastructure of considerable importance. Its university system is one of the world's largest, with more than 3 million students enrolled. India is a major publishing nation, ranking eighth in the world, and it exports books to other Third World nations as well as to the West. Finally, India is the world's second-largest producer of motion pictures, and the Indian film industry is a powerful influence within India (Indians, despite their poverty, have a high average rate of movie attendance) and has a considerable impact abroad, since Indian films are common in the Middle East and in South and Southeast Asia.

In many respects, India's knowledge and cultural industries are more autonomous than is the case in much of the Third World. Indian law forbids foreign control of many book publishers and many other industries. Multinational publishers participate in the Indian publishing business, but only as minority shareholders. This situation has increased the autonomy of Indian publishers, film studios, and newspapers. Further, India's large internal market permits publishers and others to look within the country for an audience. In most cultural and intellectual fields, India is relatively self-sufficient for expertise. There are well-trained Indian film producers and directors and a highly regarded school for training film industry personnel. There are many Indian publishers and editors, and there are several training courses for the book industry. In other words, India has achieved intellectual self-sufficiency in several important respects, and this fact separates it from many other Third World nations. Indeed, its is possible to find expatriate Indian personnel working in other parts of the Third World as teachers, editors, and in other skilled capacities.

India's intellectual and cultural infrastructure is significant in understanding its knowledge industry.[1] Although only about 40 percent of the population is literate, this figure accounts for a literate population of more than 300 million people. And while only 2 or 3 percent of the population is literate in English, this fact accounts for more than 20 million individuals, most of whom are located in the cities and are at the top of the income scales. English remains, forty years after independence, the language of the elite, of intellectual discourse in the sciences and social sciences, and as a major language of commerce. The role of English cannot be overlooked in discussing India's publishing, educational, or cultural development, yet the speakers of India's indigenous languages have also developed impressive cultural infrastructures. Hindi, the national language and mother tongue of about 45 percent of the population, is used in a growing publishing industry and in the bulk of India's films, and sustains a very large mass audience for cultural products. The speakers of Bengali, Marathi, Tamil, and Malayalam—among India's major languages—have been particularly impressive in their development of publishing houses, film studios, journals, and a lively intellectual life. Thus, while English remains the largest language for book publishing, for example, many of the other languages also support publishing houses and provide a growing audience for books, films, and magazines.

In some respects, India constitutes two major societies. Its urban sector, about 20 percent of the total, is in almost every respect fully modern, with all of the infrastructures of an industrialized society (and many of the problems as well). The 80 percent of India's population that lives in rural areas remains to be brought into the twentieth century, although elements of modern society have penetrated to the remote villages in most of India. Income, educational standards, access to goods, standards of living, and the other accoutrements of modernity are concentrated in the urban areas. The gulf between the urban minority and the rural majority is immense and remains one of India's major social problems. In this analysis, our concern is largely with the urban sector, which dominates both the production and the utilization of knowledge. It is, indeed, a special problem of Third World nations that the inequalities between urban and rural areas are very great and that this gulf is reflected in the distribution of power, wealth, and knowledge. While there are efforts to ensure that schoolbooks and the curriculum reflect the demographic realities of the nation, there is generally an urban bias in the educational system and in the mass media. This bias contributes to the migration to the cities of people seeking work and the benefits of urban life that have been exhibited in the media. Opportunities for advancement generally require a gravitation to the urban areas. Publishing and the mass media are largely urban oriented. The bulk of the market is in the cities, where literacy rates are higher, where there is access to books and other cultural products, and where there is a higher standard of living.

India, therefore, constitutes a particularly fertile example for an examination of knowledge creation and distribution. While it shares with other Third World nations poverty, low levels of literacy, and other problems, it has at the same time developed an impressive knowledge industry. Thus, it is possible to study in the Indian context both the problems of underdevelopment and the ways in which publishing and the mass media have grown in a Third World nation.

It should also be pointed out that India in some respects stands between the peripheral position of many smaller Third World nations and the metropolitan centers of the United States, Britain, or France.[2] While dependent on Western academic systems for basic research in many fields, and while looking to the West for major journals and books, India also has a large and active academic system that produces research, journals, and textbooks of its own. This knowledge often reaches other Third World nations. Similarly, Indian films, popular magazines, and other cultural products also reach a considerable audience in the Third World outside India. India, in a sense, is a "regional center" that provides an intellectual magnet certainly for its smaller neighbors in South Asia but also to some extent for sections of the Middle East and Southeast Asia. India's participation in agencies like UNESCO and other international groups also provides leadership. Thus while this chapter relies mainly on one country—India—for its examples, it is clear that there is relevance well beyond the case study.

INDIA AS CENTER AND PERIPHERY

India, like several other Third World nations, is both a major regional center that has considerable influence in its area and a peripheral country in terms of the international knowledge network.[3] India thus provides media leadership as well as cultural products to countries in the region—Bangladesh, Sri Lanka, Nepal, and to a lesser extent Pakistan and Burma. Indian films and books have an even wider influence. Many Middle Eastern, African, and Southeast Asian nations use Indian college-level textbooks extensively (in English), and Indian films are widespread in Africa and Asia. India, as a leader of the nonaligned nations, also has regional influence as a voice for South Asian concerns.

India is the largest media market in South Asia and thus has the regional offices of many multinational publishers, advertising agencies, press agencies, and other media-related companies. More important in the Indian case is its very large internal market which permits Indian publishers and media organizations to produce a variety of products for the local market that can be exported. Like many other regional centers in the Third World, such as Egypt, Mexico, and Argentina, a substantial local market is combined with the use of an international language that permits exports. India's internal market in English is considerable, and the English-speaking population is India's most affluent class and the class most directly involved in the international media network. The more than 20 million Indians who are literate in English are spread across the subcontinent. English continues to serve as India's de facto link language. The major newspapers are published in English, as are the influential magazines and journals. While higher education has shifted in part to the regional languages, English continues to dominate at the graduate level, and a number of prestigious universities still offer all of their instruction in

English. Thus, English remains quite important in Indian national and intellectual life. English, of course, is the key link with the outside world and the language in which book exports are sold.

Several of India's regional languages also have significant influence outside the country and contribute to India's regional importance. Tamil, the major South Indian language (which is unrelated to the Sanskrit-based northern languages), is spoken by significant minorities in Sri Lanka and in Singapore and Malaysia. Tamil films, books, and cultural products are common in these areas. Gujarati communities exist in East Africa, and materials in this language can be found in Africa. Most important, perhaps, is the influence of Hindi films throughout Asia and Africa. India, as the world's second largest producer of feature films, has a large export market in Africa and Asia. The Indian films that are popular with audiences in the Third World are escapist entertainment movies which do not require knowledge of Hindi, the language of these movies. Hindi popular films can be seen frequently in the Middle East, Southeast Asia, and in West and East Africa.

English is the major language of Indian book and magazine exports. The export market for Indian-produced textbooks, largely at the college and university level, is substantial in the Middle East and Southeast Asia. Indian books are often more relevant to the needs of Third World nations than are college textbooks produced in the industrialized nations. Indian books are also substantially less expensive than Western texts. Indian publishers, with a few exceptions, are not very active in the text export market, and thus Indian books are not circulated as widely as might be the case. Scientific books tend to be more widely used abroad than books in the humanities and social sciences. Indeed, it has been stated by Indian publishers that projected overseas sales are the margin between profit and loss for most scholarly books. The bulk of overseas sales are to academic libraries in North America, Britain, and Australia. In many cases, 30 percent or more of the sales of scholarly titles are sold abroad. The fact that virtually all scholarly books published in India are in English aids overseas circulation. The lack of overseas sales potential for books in Indian languages may inhibit book production in these languages.

India is at the same time very much at the periphery of the international knowledge network. As Jeremy Tunstall has pointed out, even its large and flourishing film industry is basically derivative of Hollywood models.[4] India depends on Western technologies for many of its media industries. Foreign news disseminated in India comes largely from the Western wire services (although Indian newspaper correspondents can be found in a few major capitals). Western books are widely available in India—and the use of English as the major means of intellectual communications makes the penetration by Western books easier. In virtually every respect, the India media industries are derivative of metropolitan models. The major Indian newsweekly, *India Today,* emulates *Time* and *Newsweek.* The major daily newspapers use the Western wire services, and they reprint columns from the *New York Times* and the *London Times.* Many Indian authors prefer to have their work published abroad because it provides greater remuneration and more recognition. This means, however, that authors must write with an international audience in mind rather than solely for an Indian readership. Scholarship is also very much linked to the international knowledge network. Research results are communicated in Western journals, and many Indian academics prefer to try to get their work published in major international journals, virtually all of which are published in the West. It is possible to discern an overreliance on Western cultural influences. For example, many of the book reviews found in the major newspapers and review media are of books published in the West. This means that Indian published books get insufficient attention even within India. Authors, journalists, and intellectuals all too often look abroad for validation of their work.

India occupies a position that is both central and peripheral. India is an intellectual and media power in its own right and has regional influence, yet it remains tied to the international knowledge system. The tensions between an emerging independent cultural and scientific establishment and the very strong pull of the metropolitan center are evident in much of Indian scholarship and commentary. All too often, however, Indian intellectuals function in this situation of ambivalence and conflict without conscious recognition of the problems.[5] The entire knowledge system—from the film industry that looks to the West for innovations in the technology of filmmaking to the academic community that is connected to methodological and research trends in the industrialized nations—relates to the metropolitan centers. Yet, in the context of this relationship there is also a strong element of independence. Centers and peripheries, while realities in the modern world, are nonetheless complex phenomena.

ELEMENTS OF INDEPENDENCE

This discussion emphasizes elements of the knowledge system in India that have achieved considerable independence. Few, if any, of these elements are fully independent because India has self-consciously maintained strong intellectual ties with the rest of the world and particularly with Britain and the United States. Yet, there are aspects of the system that have achieved considerable independence. These elements of independence will be useful guides to other Third World nations as they seek to build up their own capabilities in the field of knowledge production and distribution.

Infrastructures

Because of a considerable investment over time, the existence of a pool of trained manpower, and the large internal market, most elements of the Indian knowledge and media industries have basic self-sufficiency in both personnel and equipment. What is more, training facilities exist within India for most media fields, and an increasing proportion of the hardware, from printing presses to film and paper-making capacity, is locally produced. When compared to other Third World nations, these capabilities are quite impressive. A few examples will illustrate this point.

The Indian publishing industry is self-sufficient in most respects, although the most advanced technologies in printing equipment and computer-assisted typesetting must still be imported from abroad. In terms of personnel, most editors and other professionals in India are locally trained. Several training courses exist in Indian colleges for publishing personnel, and many publishers provide on-the-job training as well. Training courses for printers are also offered. Virtually no expatriates can be found anywhere in the publishing or printing industries in India. India produces its own printing presses, although it does not manufacture the most advanced equipment. Indian-produced printing presses are outmoded on the world market but are still useful in the domestic printing industry. As India has moved into competition in printing and publishing on the world market, it has found that some kinds of up-to-date equipment must be imported from abroad. For example, India now exports typesetting to other countries, and, in general, this typesetting is done on imported computer-assisted equipment. Low wages and overhead permit India to compete effectively in this area. The equipment, however, must be imported, although India is now producing its own software in some fields. It is a curious paradox that the needs of the local publishing and printing industries can be fulfilled from indigenously manufactured items, but when the nation moves to participate in the international market, state-of-the-art, imported equipment is needed.

Paper is a key ingredient of the publishing industry and is an often-ignored element in knowledge distribution generally, since without an adequate paper supply at a price that is congruent with local purchasing power, access to many kinds of knowledge is inhibited. India is ahead of many Third World nations in that it does have a significant papermaking capacity. But Indian-made paper is expensive, is in short supply, and is especially inadequate for book manufacturing. "Cultural paper," the kind of paper generally used for books, is of poor quality, and in very short supply in India. The Indian government has discouraged paper imports as a means of building the local industry and conserving foreign exchange.[6] Thus, there are recurring shortages, high prices, and problems of quality in book paper. Newsprint is less of a problem in India, and most Indian newspapers are printed on locally produced paper. Despite the problems, the existence of a domestic printing industry is an important advantage for India. Many other Third World nations are completely dependent on foreign paper suppliers located almost exclusively in the industrial nations.[7] Thus, prices for paper, as well as the nature and quality of the paper, are controlled by the industrial countries.

The Indian film industry is also largely self-sufficient in terms of personnel training and in most aspects of film production. High-quality technicolor film is often imported, but India does produce films of many kinds domestically. Sophisticated cameras are still imported as well. But most Indian films, from documentaries to large-budget popular films, are made entirely in India by Indian personnel with an increasing proportion of Indian-made equipment. Indian film studios are well equipped.[8] By Western standards, Indian films are not terribly sophisticated, but they suit a large audience in India and abroad, and they are relatively inexpensive to produce. Further, filmmakers like Mrinal Sen and Satyajit Ray have proved that the Indian film industry can produce high-quality films.

Textbooks

The provision of school textbooks to the educational system is a key contribution of any publishing industry, since texts are a key to learning and, in many countries, just as important as teachers.[9] India provides virtually all of its textbook needs at all levels. With fifteen official languages and with schools in many of the Indian states functioning in several languages, the provision of textbooks is a considerable challenge. Yet, India has developed texts in all fields in more than fifteen languages. In most cases, these texts reflect Indian curricular concepts and use examples from India, although theoretical aspects often stem from Western research and development. In most states, textbooks at the primary and secondary levels are provided by state textbook agencies, which sometimes work with private-sector publishers to produce the books and sometimes have this capability themselves. The takeover of textbook publishing by the states has been a serious problem for private-sector publishers since it has removed one of their most lucrative and predictable markets. At the college and university levels India also provides for the bulk of its textbook needs, usually through the private sector. In some fields, especially at the graduate level, books must still be imported or printed in India under license from foreign publishers.

In most fields Indian authors are able to produce appropriate textbooks, and the publishing industry is sufficiently well-developed to provide the technical expertise to produce the books. Indian textbooks are generally more inexpensively produced than their Western counterparts, in keeping with the fiscal realities of the Indian educational system. It has been an impressive accomplishment in the postindependence period to develop the infrastructures, the knowledge, and the skills to produce textbooks in a range of fields in many languages. It should also be kept in mind that close to 100 million Indians attend school at any given time, and while there are still shortages of books in many fields—and particularly in the rural areas—the Indian textbook industry has developed impressively.

Authors

With the world's eighth-largest publishing industry, India has developed a large population of authors in all of its publishing languages. While there are as yet very few Indians who can support themselves fully by writing, there is expertise in India to produce books on most subjects, and there are incentives for authors. Although India still imports textbooks from abroad at the university level, virtually all texts at the primary and secondary levels are written by Indians, as well as an increasing proportion at the post-secondary level. Academics write research-based monographs, and there is a market for such books within India and to some extent abroad. Popular novels, self-help books, and other kinds of books are also produced in large numbers in India. Without question, the most remunerative language in which to write is English (with the exception of a few blockbuster Hindi novels); thus many authors prefer to publish their books in English. Several of the regional languages, however, have developed sizable audiences in recent years, and authors have come forward to serve these emerging markets. Bengali, Marathi, Malayalam, and Telegu have emerged as languages of significant book production. Hindi, the official language of the country, also has a growing book market, and of greater importance, government sponsorship for some book publication.

Television

The emergence of television in the past decade as a major force in India has brought major changes to the media industry. At present, most of the major urban areas have access to television, and the large metropolitan areas now have color reception. Some rural areas are provided with satellite-assisted television reception for educational purposes. The television networks, controlled by the central government, have created new jobs in writing, acting, producing, and ancillary skills. Virtually all these jobs are located in the major cities and are available to people with high levels of education.

As India entered the television age, it was interested in avoiding some of the errors of other Third World nations. As a result, only a small portion of television time in India is devoted to foreign-produced material. While there has been some criticism of the showing of noneducational Hindi popular films on television, most of the programming is indigenous and some of it rather innovative. India has attempted to use television for educational purposes and has been fairly successful in extenidng programming to some of the rural areas. At present, these advanced technologies are being used only on a trial basis. The point is that while there are certainly problems in the creation of a complex television network using not only Hindi and English but also the various Indian regional languages, there has been significant progress toward providing the country with indigenous programming.

India has succeeded in developing most of the basic structures of a knowledge industry during the past thirty years. It has achieved virtual independence in textbook development, it has almost completely indigenized the publishing industry, and it has moved forcefully into the mass media area as well. There is a vigorous cultural life in virtually all of India's major indigenous languages, with major independent film industries in such languages as Tamil, Telegu, and Bengali, as well as the national industry in Hindi. While India is still very much part of the international knowledge network, it has nonetheless achieved a significant degree of independence.

INTERDEPENDENCE AND DEPENDENCE

India's ties to the international knowledge network, its heritage of colonialism, and its continued use of English are all elements of interdependence. It is useful to point to some elements of this relationship to indicate how even a large and in some ways autonomous cultural system interacts with the major metropolitan cultural empires.[10] The phenomena discussed here are only illustrative and by no means exhaustive.

The immense technological, commercial, and historical weight of the international knowledge system weighs heavily on India, as it does on the other countries of the Third World. Basic media technology is Western in nature, and the patents, licenses, and manufacturing facilities are in the industrialized nations. Although it has been pointed out that India has some capability in building printing machinery and some other media products, new technological developments come from the West and must be purchased, sometimes at considerable cost.

Satellite communications, computer-assisted typesetting, and many other innovations must be imported. India, like other developing nations, must make difficult decisions concerning what aspects of the emerging technologies to utilize. Cost-benefit analyses, the question of whether a new technology will relate effectively to existing traditional structures, and other issues are part of such decisions. The pressures to use the new technologies, almost regardless of the cost, are immense. Indeed, if India wishes to participate in international media and knowledge networks, it must keep abreast of these developments. And the origin of the new technologies and control over them remain with industrialized nations. For example, the decision whether to utilize color technology for television has far-reaching implications. One must choose a particular technology, must modify production facilities as well as transmission stations, and put in place a capability for the manufacture of color television sets (or import them at considerable cost). The pressure, internal and external, to use color technology is great.

The Western heritage in the development of the mass media is also significant and tends to tie Third World nations to continuing relationships with Western knowledge networks.[11] A few examples will indicate the power of this heritage. The concept of the book is a Western concept; it was exported to the Third World. Not only was modern printing and paper technology a Western invention, but the concept of how books should be printed, what quality of paper should be used, and other factors were also imported from the West. It might be that different ideas about books, such as the possible usefulness of printing inexpensive volumes that have a short life, would be more useful for the Third World than the traditional Western concept that a book should be relatively durable.[12] Similarly, Indian magazines and newspapers look very much like their Western counterparts. Their purposes are similar, journalistic conventions are common, and there is a great deal of borrowing from Western models. As noted earlier, the Indian print media use articles and stories from the Western wire services. Further, Western publications such as *Time* and *Newsweek* have a wide circulation in India. Even *Reader's Digest*, which is published in an Indian edition, ranks as one of the most important publications in the country.

India is an integral part of the international knowledge system. It is a party to the international copyright agreements, and although there has been much criticism in India of copyright arrangements and some "pirating" of popular books, India nonetheless has maintained allegiance to the copyright system.[13] The copyright system is controlled by the industrialized nations, and despite some liberalization in recent years, it basically serves their needs. Third World nations such as India have some difficulties obtaining permission to reprint or translate books published originally in the West, and the cost of obtaining rights is sometimes high. India has relatively little to offer the industrialized nations in terms of book translations or rights, and so the intellectual balance of payments is quite one-sided. Further, while India does export books to both Third World and industrialized nations, it imports many more books than it exports. The prices of books are determined in the West, and those prices are very often quite high. In many areas, such as research, science, and technology, virtually all of the relevant books are published in the West.

India is also part of the international commercial network of knowledge. It depends on the world market—with prices and terms dictated by the producer (industrialized) nations. The major book distribution agencies are in the West, and they determine the terms and conditions of the book trade. Many Western publishers have representatives or branch offices in India, while few Indian publishers have offices abroad. Indian newspapers subscribe to the Western wire services, but no Western agencies have much interest in the Press Trust of India. Thus, India is part of the system, but in almost every respect it does not determine how the system works. Book prices are set abroad. The costs of participation in worldwide communications systems are also externally controlled.

Western nations also attempt to influence and sometimes control the knowledge and media industries in the Third World.[14] Foreign-aid programs often have a component relating to books and the mass media. It has been common for industrialized nations to provide textbooks in large quantities to Third World nations, thus causing problems of adjustment for local publishing industries and influencing students through these books. Some nations have provided special assistance for book exports to the Third World. Information agencies frequently seek to influence elites through publications and other media-related activities. Seldom are there similar activities by Third World nations in the industrialized countries.

The heritage of the colonial language and the continuing use of that language is also a matter of considerable importance for the Third World. About half of India's books are published in English, although only 2 or 3 percent of the population is literate in that language. Similarly, the major daily newspapers and magazines are also in English. The use of English by the elite has meant that a very large proportion of the Indian population is cut off from an important knowledge distribution network. Despite some official efforts to disseminate knowledge through the regional languages, the dominance of English has not changed. The participation of India in the international network reinforces the role of English within India, since the network functions in English.

It can be seen from this discussion that in many respects India does not control its own destiny in terms of knowledge distribution and creation. Because it must import some technologies—the results of research done overseas—and because it must rely on information from the industrialized nations, India remains dependent in significant ways on external forces. It does not control the prices it must pay for many of these elements. And it does not control the mechanisms for distribution, so it remains at the mercy of the industrialized nations.

CENTERS AND PERIPHERIES WITHIN INDIA

It is tempting to treat nations as single entities and to generalize about them. Yet India is a complex country with considerable regional variations and with a gulf between the relatively advanced urban areas (about 20 perent of the total) and the countryside. While many of these differences are magnified in the Indian context, they are common in the Third World and very often ignored in analyses of Third World realities. In India, the urban areas, and particularly the major metropolitan cities, are centers and the rural areas are peripheral. Knowledge emanates from the center and generally reflects an urban orientation. The publishing houses, media producers, major universities, and most authors are urban centered. Urban values, life styles, concerns, occupational structures, and interests dominate the media. Urban income levels are higher and therefore media products are almost exclusively aimed at the urban market.

Further, rural areas find access to knowledge and cultural products difficult. Radio reaches much of the country, but television is largely limited to the larger cities. In many rural areas, electrical supplies are sporadic at best. There are few bookstores, and mail service may be somewhat irregular. Literacy rates are significantly lower in the countryside, and, as has been noted, income levels are lower. Indian authorities have been concerned about this dramatic imbalance, and efforts have been made in some areas, such as the images found in textbooks, to reflect more accurately the urban-rural mix in India.

Regions are also unequally provided with access to the knowledge system. India's more widely spoken languages generally are better covered by books, magazines, and other cultural products. A few regions with strong cultural interests, such as Bengal and Maharashtra, are particularly well served. Some parts of the country, however, have relatively less access to the knowledge network. Some of the poorer states, such as Bihar, and a few linguistic groups, such as Assamese, Sindhis, Oriyas, and a few others, are relatively underserved in terms of books and journals.

It goes almost without saying that income levels are differentially served by the knowledge network. Those with higher incomes are dramatically overserved. The urban middle and upper classes have the best access, and most media products are aimed at these groups. Even India's flourishing film magazines are aimed at this economic group. The advertising industry, which is an important part of the economic base for newspapers and magazines, is aimed at this very small (probably under 10 percent) portion of the Indian population. And with the very great gulf in India (as in many other Third World nations) between the relatively wealthy minority and the impoverished masses, the differences in access to the knowledge network are dramatic.

In every country there are internal variations—by class, region, language, or other variables. But in India the gulf between the centers and the peripheries within the nation is very dramatic indeed. The danger, of course, is that the mass of the population will be cut off from the cultural mainstream and that resentments may develop as a result. Further, the implications for literacy campaigns, educational programs, and the like are immense. Within a country like India it is impossible to posit national generalizations because of the dramatic variations among the regions. One must first explore the centers and peripheries within the country and explain the differing access to and participation in the knowledge system of the nation.

This discussion has dealt almost exclusively with the infrastructures and networks of knowledge distribution and creation and not with the content of the information that is transmitted. Such an analysis involves a complex consideration of the content of school textbooks, video images, the content of journals and newspapers, and a range of other sources of information reaching Indians and is beyond the scope of this paper. Suffice it to say that the information received by Indians, who in this respect are somewhat typical of Third World peoples, comes from a variety of sources. It is likely that the information reaching the rural majority is largely of indigenous origins. Schoolbooks are authored by Indians using Indian data and examples. The basic content of radio and television is largely indigenous. The daily newspapers depend on Indian sources for news and analysis of South Asian affairs but still must use Western information for much of their foreign news and commentary. Even the indigenous-language newspapers use Western news sources translated into Indian languages. Information sources and content for the better-educated urban minority come from more complex origins. Serious journals often use articles written by Westerners. Western newsmagazines, such as *Time* and *Newsweek*, have significant readerships in India. At the college and university level, foreign textbooks are widely used, and even indigenously produced volumes have Western models and sources in many fields. Western scholars have produced much of the research about India, and their interpretations are widely accepted, although the balance of scholarship is changing.

India has had a relatively open attitude concerning the importation of knowledge. Educated Indians have ready access to information from abroad, and books, videotapes, magazines, and other artifacts of foreign knowledge and culture are highly valued, yet the balance has been slowly changing as Indians have produced more information, knowledge, and the elements of modern culture. There is a mingling of indigenous and foreign sources, even in the products produced by Indians. There is an inevitable borrowing of knowledge and styles in a world where the dominant cultural and educational patterns are largely produced in the West in the major world languages.

India's knowledge distribution apparatus is complex and has elements of both dependence and self-sufficiency. India is an intellectual power in its region, yet it depends in many ways on the industrialized nations. India has, in its knowledge system, elements that come from both the center and the periphery. The elements that go to make up the knowledge system—colonial heritage, the continued use of English as a key language, the power of the international Western-dominated media, and strong and vibrant national publishing and media industries—exist in a complex and changing relationship. The purpose of this chapter has been to point precisely to this complexity. Without question, India, as one of the largest and most powerful of the emerging powers of the Third World, will have a key role to play in the intellectual balance of power in the twenty-first century. Its publishing and film industries are already powerful forces in the Third World, yet it is clear from this discussion that even a nation as large as India faces real problems in building an independent knowledge system.

The role of emerging technologies creates an even more ambivalent situation in the near future. As India and other Third World nations are increasingly linked to technology-driven international knowledge networks, it is clear that control will remain basically with the Western media empires. India at least is aware of the problems and is trying, as with its television programming, to maximize the indigenous content of its offerings. The challenges are daunting. It may be useful to point to some possible ways in which Third World nations may maximize their independence and autonomy within the context of the international system.

1. National policies may help to concentrate scarce resources in areas that can maximize strengths. The key term here may be *selectivity*—if it is not possible to build a fully independent knowledge system, at least a segment of that system can be autonomous. For example, National Book Development Councils, which exist in many Third World nations, help to focus attention and policies.

2. Regional cooperation may be a means of maximizing autonomy among Third World nations. To date, efforts at regional cooperation have not succeeded, but the concept remains a powerful one.

3. Combined action to force alterations in international policies that work against the interest of Third World nations, such as the international copyright agreements, is one likely option.

4. Awareness of the problems will help national policies—and the individual actions of agencies—maximize autonomy. For example, particular foreign-aid policies of the industrialized nations may not be in

> the best interests of the Third World. By careful analysis, such policies may be stopped.

There is no panacea in a world of complexities in which power is not equally distributed. The basic control over the international knowledge system will remain in the hands of the technologically advanced nations with large academic systems, the means of control over the communications network, and the bulk of investment capital, yet as India has shown, there is within this context much that can be done to maximize autonomy and independence. Those Third World nations that have built up effective knowledge networks, such as India, Mexico, and Egypt, have a special responsibility to work in the interests of their smaller compeers. In a world of inequality, knowledge is at least a commodity that can be partly manipulated so that a measure of independence an autonomy may be achieved.

Chapter 5

Higher Education and International Knowledge Distribution

Universities are among the world's most important producers of knowledge. They are also crucial links in the chain of knowledge distribution, yet few have analyzed their role in the knowledge distribution enterprise. University presses, particularly in the United States and Britain, are major publishers of scientific literature. Scholarly journals are typically edited in universities and are frequently published on campus. Academic institutions are also the primary users of scholarly publications of all kinds. Journals would not survive without the library market, and the products of the university presses are sold mainly to academic libraries. Individual scholars as well as libraries are consumers of the various newly established data bases and bibliographical services.

The knowledge distribution system also has important international implications. Academic institutions in many countries are frequently linked by their participation in an international system of knowledge distribution. Universities in the large industrialized nations, particularly in the United States, Britain, France, and, to a lesser extent, West Germany and the Soviet Union, are the major producers of scholarly knowledge, as well as the main distributors. Academic institutions in other countries, particularly in the Third World, are largely consumers of scholarly materials and research produced elsewhere. Knowledge systems have centers and peripheries in the production and distribution of knowledge. As already discussed, the flow of knowledge is largely from the "centers" to the "peripheries."[1]

I am concerned here with describing and analyzing the role of higher education in the system of knowledge distribution throughout the world.[2] It is not enough to produce knowledge through research and scholarship; there must also be the means to disseminate that knowledge so that users may have access to it. Universities must be aware of their key—and very complex—role in the dissemination process, and recognize their responsibilities in this area.

The knowledge system is at present under considerable pressure.[3] The new technologies, especially repography in all its forms and particularly the ubiquitous photocopying machines, cause economic and ethical problems as well as facilitating immediate access to information in many fields. Data bases have dramatically expanded the horizons of scholars, but libraries have also had problems dealing with the new technological advances. The spiraling cost of scholarly books and journals has created problems for both the producers and the users. The proliferation of journals has meant that academic libraries now spend more money on serials than on books. While the expansion of knowledge is a challenge to scholars in all fields and in all countries, it is a particularly severe problem in the Third World, where access to an expanding knowledge basis is very difficult. Moreover, fiscal problems for higher education in many countries have meant that budgets for the dissemination and storage of knowledge—especially library funds and allocations for university presses—have been cut. We are therefore concerned here with a very complex set of relationships.

The role of higher educational institutions in knowledge distribution is both formal and informal. Universities, through the system of evaluation of professorial performance, act as indirect gatekeepers, deciding what kinds of knowledge will be rewarded. Libraries, through their decisions on acquisitions, also have a role in determining what kinds of knowledge are economically viable.[4] Academic institutions with university presses have formal means of publishing and distributing knowledge. Universities frequently publish journals sponsored by departments, faculties, or other academic agencies. These journals are key elements in the knowledge distribution system. In short, universities have a multiple role in shaping the nature and scope of knowledge distribution. They are the home of the many "invisible colleges" of scholars and researchers that are the core of any academic discipline.[5]

This chapter considers new technologies, traditional academic practices and norms, an international system, and the direct and indirect roles of academic institutions in one of the most important, yet very frequently ignored, functions of higher education. It discusses both the institutional factors and the human dimensions of knowledge distribution and higher education.

THE INTERNATIONAL KNOWLEDGE NETWORK

Knowledge knows no borders. It is freely circulated internationally even when governments attempt to restrict its flow. The development of an international network of knowledge distribution is by no means a new phenomenon. Medieval European universities functioned in Latin, the international scholarly lingua franca of the time, and knowledge circulated throughout the continent through manuscripts as well as scholars.[6] In East Asia, Chinese served as the major language of scholarship for many centuries, bringing religious, scientific, and philosophical knowledge to Japan and Southeast Asia. Academic "centers" have always existed. Many of the American scholars who were responsible for the growth of the research university in the United States were trained in Germany, the academic center of the late nineteenth century.[7] At that time a knowledge of German was necessary to keep abreast of scientific knowledge, and the major German academic journals were the primary means of disseminating new research. Thus centers and peripheries existed in both the Middle Ages and in the nineteenth century.[8] It is also possible for academic institutions within one country to move from a position of central prominence to one of lesser importance and back again. Oxford University was never far from the center of British society but did not play a key scholarly role for a long period prior to the nineteenth century.[9]

In the contemporary world, a truly international knowledge network has emerged which for the first time covers most of the globe. Research done in the major academic centers has influence in other countries. Modern technology has permitted the global emergence of a knowledge network, and only political constraints at times interfere with this network.[10]

Inequality is one hallmark of international knowledge dissemination. The emergence of English as the major language of science and scholarship in the post–World War II period is one of the most important elements in the contemporary knowledge network. The bulk of the world's scholarly journals are published in English, and the Anglo-American universities spend more than half of the world's total academic budgets for research and development. Twelve nations have English as their native language and another thirty-three countries use it as a major medium of communication.[11] Of course, French continues to play an important international role, and Russian is prominent in Eastern Europe. But knowledge dissemination, whether through journals and books or at international conferences, is increasingly communicated in English. This situation gives the countries that use English a considerable advantage. English is the Latin of the twentieth century and is firmly entrenched as the major language of scholarship and research.

The fact that the major publishers of books and journals, most of the editors, the major research laboratories and libraries, and the very large majority of the key scientists are in a small number of industrialized nations means that these nations, and the universities in them, have a dominant role in the dissemination system. These same countries produce most of the world's research. The journal editors, publishers, and libraries of the North dominate the system because of the weight of their resources. The universities and research institutions of the industrialized nations have, in a sense, a stranglehold over the production of knowledge.

Technological developments tend to reinforce these inequalities by further centralizing the knowledge system. Data bases, without exception, originate in the industrialized nations, use information from these nations, and are disseminated throughout the world, often earning a profit for those who control the network. The ERIC system in the United States, using federal government funds, serves academic libraries and the research community. The Online Computer Library Center (OCLC) bibliographic system is also university based for the most part. These new tools for knowledge dissemination and retrieval are very important. Satellite communications networks, fibre-optic computer systems, and the like all serve an increasingly international audience, but again are controlled from the centers and disseminated to the peripheries. Perhaps the only new technology which has lent itself to independent use is that of reprography—the photocopying revolution. Here the technology is relatively widely diffused and has permitted nonproducing countries to copy materials quickly, sometimes violating the international copyright regulations.[12]

Knowledge concerns technology, but it is also a matter of highly skilled people. Here again, the metropolitan centers have a major advantage over the peripheries. Most of the world's prominent researchers are confined to a small number of premier universities in the industrialized nations. These are the scholars who produce the research, serve as evaluators for journals and publishers, and constitute the bulk of the invisible colleges of the disciplines. In many Third World nations, there are few skilled personnel to edit manuscripts, to coordinate the activities of publishing books and journals, or to develop and maintain academic libraries.

There is an increasing international flow of students, researchers, and others involved in higher education. There are, for example, more than 335,000 foreign students studying in American colleges and universities. Most are from the Third World, and many will return to academic institutions and research laboratories in their home countries. They will imbibe the norms, values, and orientations of American higher education during their stay, and they will become part of an international network that looks toward its American alma maters for cues.[13] Many thousands of foreign students study in France (which has a higher proportion of foreign students than does the United States), Britain, West Germany, Czechoslovakia, the Soviet Union, and other industrialized nations. The Fulbright Program, its West German counterpart, the Deutsche Akademische Austauschdienst (DAAD), and a variety of other agencies send scholars around the world in unprecedented numbers. These individuals become part of the international knowledge network by imparting skills, working with colleagues overseas, and developing institutional and personal links.

The impact of research and publication reinforces the status quo. In a study of articles published in the sciences, a number of generalizations were found. In 1973, the industrialized nations accounted for 84 percent of the total scientific articles published. American authors alone accounted for 43 percent of the articles, and Western Europe took second place with 17 percent. The entire Third World accounted for only 5 percent of the total. As Eugene Garfield put it, "Western journals control the flow of international communication almost as much as Western news agencies 'monopolize' international news."[14]

Financial resources are a crucial part of the knowledge network. Money is needed to operate a publishing house or journal, to pay editors, and to underwrite research. The academic institutions themselves must have adequate financing—and just as importantly, they must devote their resources to research and dissemination. Furthermore, there need to be adequate markets for the products of knowledge, and these exist largely in the industrialized nations. An edition of 1,000 copies of a scholarly book can be sold in the United States although sometimes with difficulty, but not in many smaller nations. The larger industrialized nations have an adequate internal market for scholarly materials and can build their exports on the basis of this domestic market. Other nations do not have this luxury. Knowledge dissemination, particularly at the esoteric levels of specialized research, is never profitable and must frequently be subsidized. In the United States, research grants often provide funds for dissemination of research results. These grants in turn permit journals to levy page charges as a way of paying for publication costs. The university presses are often subsidized by their sponsoring academic institutions. Academic institutions in the wealthy industrialized nations can afford to provide well-stocked academic libraries, to subscribe to the key journals of the world, to ensure that information is readily available to researchers and students, and in general to maintain an adequate dissemination apparatus on campus. This is not necessarily the case in many smaller, poorer, and less well-endowed institutions and nations. Indeed, in many respects, the wealthier institutions and nations gain enhanced advantages because they are better able to keep up with the expanding knowledge base.

In the physical and biological sciences, where laboratories and increasingly expensive scientific equipment are necessary for research, the stranglehold of the major industrialized nations is especially strong. The infrastructures of science in fields requiring such costly instruments are possible only in wealthy nations that emphasize research and development. Since funds for scientific infrastructures come mainly from government sources, scientific research is often geared toward the research interests of governmental bodies and thus reflects, at least in part, specific policy orientations rather than the direct research interests of the scholarly community. In this respect, the governments of the major industrialized nations exercise an immense influence on the direction of research and scientific productivity.

Academic institutions are at the heart of the international knowledge network. In many ways, they can be international institutions with students and staff from many countries. The libraries of such institutions are repositories of materials in many languages and from many countries. Some larger universities develop their own foreign relations, with links to overseas institutions, spheres of influence, and the like. Again, the major research-based universities of the industrialized nations tend to dominate these relationships, with Third World institutions acting as junior partners.

There are, of course, centers and peripheries among academic institutions within nations, and the relationships described here are by no means limited to the international sphere. Universities with fewer resources, smaller libraries, less adequate access to external funding, and small laboratories are on the peripheries. Such institutions generally do not house the major scholarly journals and do not have access to the center of the academic marketplace. They frequently feel their peripheral status and attempt, usually with only mixed results, to move closer to the centers and hence to the sources of intellectual resources, power, and prestige.

UNIVERSITIES AS PUBLISHERS

Universities are publishers, and as such are direct contributors to the knowledge dissemination system.[15] The most direct and obvious publishing activity of a university is that of the university press.[16] But academic staff may engage in publishing activities on their own. Universities frequently subsidize the publication of books by commercial publishers or other agencies. In short, the involvement of many large academic institutions in publishing is quite significant—and is in general unanalyzed or even unknown to the institutions.

Although the university presses are responsible for only somewhat more than 1 percent of the total income of American publishers and a somewhat higher proportion of the title output, their impact on scholarly publishing is substantial.[17] For the scholar, the university presses are at the top of the prestige hierarchy. The university presses, because of their nonprofit status and their traditional orientations, are able to publish scholarly monographs and research studies that would be difficult or impossible for private sector publishers to issue. University presses, like the academic institutions that sponsor them, are largely meritocratic agencies that make publishing decisions to some extent free of the commercial constraints of other publishers. They see their roles as related to the advancement of knowledge, and they frequently publish manuscripts which may not be viable in the commercial sector.[18]

The American university presses have been faced with difficult problems during the fiscal constraints and other problems of the last decade. As the prices of books increased and library budgets declined, average sales dropped at the same time that institutional support was cut back because of financial pressure. External funding for scholarly publishing also declined. This combination of circumstances spelled major difficulties for the university presses. Several closed, and the number of titles published annually declined significantly. Most of the presses, however, survived and are now relatively healthy, although long-term trends are difficult to predict.

While the economics of the university presses differs from that of commercial publishers because they are nonprofit entities and are not subject to taxes, they are nonetheless part of the economic marketplace of publishing. Rising costs of production and steady or decreasing library sales (most university press books are purchased by institutions) have placed pressures on the university presses. Institutional sponsors have been less willing to provide subsidies to their presses. The university publishers have to some extent become more commercial in their orientation, searching for manuscripts that will sell in the marketplace. Some have even published cookbooks.

The university presses are also an important part of the international knowledge network. Academic libraries and scholars abroad find that the products of the American university presses are important. The presses help to disseminate American scholarship abroad. However, very few books by foreign authors are published by these presses, so the traffic in knowledge is mostly one way. There are some exceptions to this generalization. Ohio University Press distributes scholarly books from Southeast Asia, the University of California Press has a distinguished list of Asian books, including many Asian authors, and Princeton University Press has had a long relationship with the University of Tokyo Press. But in general, the American university presses tend to be rather insular.

The university press is more important in the United States as a source of scholarly books than it is in any other country. Even in England, where Oxford and Cambridge university presses established the tradition of academic publishing, only a few of the other universities have presses. It must be kept in mind that both Oxford and Cambridge, while they publish many scholarly books, are also publishers of textbooks, atlases, bibles, and other nonscholarly items. They are not university presses in the American sense. In Canada and Australia, there are a small number of university presses, and some have been established in Japan, Malaysia, Nigeria, and other countries. In most of Europe, however, academic publishing is done by private-sector publishers and not by the universities. In the Soviet Union, scholarly publishing is largely a responsibility of the various institutes of the prestigious Academies of Sciences, although Moscow University Press recently celebrated its 225th anniversary.[19]

The links between the university presses in the United States and their sponsoring institutions and their faculties are frequently rather distant. University administrators have a vague commitment to the press because it has traditionally been supported by the institution and is the source of considerable prestige.[20] But, for the most part, their understanding of the role of the press and of its problems is very limited. The institution's faculty members are similarly distanced from the press. Some of their books are published by it, but few have any real understanding of its problems or role in the broader knowledge system.

The university press is the most visible element of a university's publishing role, but it is not the only one. American academic institutions engage in a wide range of publishing activities. Many departments, centers, or schools have monograph or occasional paper series, some of which are quite extensive and successful. These series may be quite important in a particular scholarly field and may have an international reputation. They are frequently published without a great deal of expertise and are usually heavily subsidized, frequently without very clear fiscal accountability. These semiformal publishing activities are seldom subject to university scrutiny, and there is no central record keeping. Distribution of these publications tends to be particularly deficient, since the departments or centers issuing them have neither the expertise nor the staff to effectively publicize and distribute their series. These publishing efforts, which might be called the "ephemeral" publishing activities of universities, are probably quite significant in scope. They need closer scrutiny, help with production and distribution, and in general a more coordinated effort.

Universities also engage in other publishing activities. Books are sometimes sponsored or subsidized by academic institutions. Many colleges and universities have funds available to help faculty members get their manuscripts published. Institutions may lend their names to the publishing activities of private-sector publishers. Individual faculty members may use university facilities as they engage in publishing activities. It is not unusual, for example, for humanities professors to "self-publish" their own or their colleagues' writing with the assistance of academic departments and using university facilities. Again, the institution seldom is aware of these activities. The more prestigious institutions in the United States engage in a wider range of publishing activities than the others, but publishing seems fairly widespread in the American academic system.

THE ROLE OF JOURNALS

Scholarly journals in most fields—particularly in the sciences—are the key element in the knowledge distribution network, and are even more important than books. Even in an age of computer-based data networks, journals are the standard means of communicating the latest knowledge in most academic fields. In some fields in the medical sciences, journals have been linked up with computer networks to provide instantaneous communications, and this change has meant that journal users do not have to wait for the usual lag in publication. In general, the traditional scholarly journal continues to flourish, relatively untouched by the technological revolution (except for using, in many cases, computer-assisted composing facilities). Scholarly journals are, with few exceptions, dependent on institutions of higher education for their survival. It is not an exaggeration to state that without the support, direct and indirect, of academic institutions, all scholarly journals would collapse. Thus, it is important to look closely at the relationship between scholarly journal and universities.

Academic libraries are the major purchasers of scholarly journals. In the United States, three-quarters or more of the circulation of research and scholarly journals goes to libraries. Of the most expensive journals in the medical and scientific areas, libraries are virtually the only buyers. The economic impact of the academic libraries is even greater, since most journals charge a significantly higher subscription rate to libraries than to individuals. It is not unusual for 90 percent of a journal's income to be generated by libraries. Libraries are also more reliable purchasers, since they regularly renew their subscriptions and can be counted on for a long-term commitment. It is no exaggeration to say that academic institutions, through their libraries, are the economic backbone of the large majority of scholarly journals.

Academic institutions are important to journals in other ways as well. Most of the authors of scholarly articles are teachers or researchers in colleges and universities. Their institutions directly subsidize authorship in many ways. They provide incentives to write for publication through the promotion and reward systems of American higher education. It might be pointed out that academic systems with less direct emphasis on publication as a condition for employment or promotion generally have lower levels of scholarly writing and activity. Academic institutions also provide favorable conditions for scholarly publication through secretarial and other support facilities that are offered to their staff. In sum, universities provide a congenial institutional environment in which to produce scholarly writing. At least for untenured staff in the United States, the sanctions for not producing scholarly writing are also considerable.[21]

In sponsoring academic journals, universities provide office space, secretarial support, and encouragement. In many countries, sponsorship of a scholarly journal is seen to lend prestige to the university. Scholarly editors are for the most part professors in universities, and they are frequently given released time to devote to their editorial responsibilities. In some instances, the institution often provides a direct financial subsidy to a journal as well as the usual indirect support given to nonsponsored publications. In the United States, several venerable journals which were under financial pressure were rescued by universities. The *Partisan Review,* for many years an independent journal, was sponsored by Boston University in an effort to keep it alive in a period of fiscal crisis. Other universities helped save independent literary and critical journals which found it difficult to survive in the inflationary period of the 1960s. The universities benefitted from the prestige of the journal, and their faculties found it stimulating to work with the publications. With few exceptions, the academic sponsors have permitted a great deal of intellectual freedom to their journals, and in general the relationship seems to be mutually beneficial.[22] It is possible, however, that the professorial editors of the journals are less innovative and imaginative than the young independent intellectuals of an earlier day who founded the journals and managed them through difficult days. The fact is that American universities now sponsor many of the most successful of the "little magazines" that contribute significantly to the development of American creative writing and literary criticism.

University presses are also significant publishers of scholarly journals. The University of Chicago Press, probably the largest of the academic publishers of journals, is responsible for more than forty journals in a dozen fields of scholarship. A number of American university presses publish journals, sometimes specializing in one or two disciplines. The university presses provide support services, financial stability, technical expertise, and frequently a measure of prestige to the journals. Some presses publish journals which are associated exclusively with their university, but frequently they issue a wider range of publications. In some instances, the press "owns" the journal, while in other circumstances, the journals are owned by scholarly societies or academic departments. The presses frequently find the journal business profitable, since it is more predictable than book publishing and is a way of publicizing books and other publishing activities.

The publication of a scholarly journal does not require a massive financial investment, but it does take considerable expertise.[23] The technical aspects of journal publication, such as maintaining subscription lists, arranging for composition, mailing, and related functions are generally beyond the capability of academic editors, who have neither the time nor the expertise to handle the details of publication. Links with a publisher, sometimes a university press but often a commercial press, provide the needed technical expertise to permit the successful operation of a scholarly journal.

Universities are even more important to scholarly journals in some other countries than they are in the United States. This is particularly true in the developing nations of the Third World, where the infrastructures of publishing are very limited and editorial expertise is scarce.[24] Third World academic institutions frequently sponsor scholarly journals as a means of providing outlets for the publications of their faculties, of building up an indigenous tradition of scholarship, and of communicating knowledge about the country to an external audience. The financial and staff commitments to these journals are relatively significant, since costs of production are high and academic budgets very limited. Local markets for scholarly publications are also limited. Nevertheless, journals are seen as a high priority, and it is usually more practical to publish a journal than to issue scholarly books.

In Western Europe, the universities play less of a role in both scholarly publishing and journal publishing than in the United States or the Third World. Most scholarly journals are issued by private-sector publishers. The universities, of course, provide the editors and the indirect support for editorial offices in much the same way as in the United States. The academic library market constitutes the largest and most lucrative source of subscribers. However, in most European countries, it seems that scholarly journals have a larger individual market, and since there are fewer universities, the institutional market is smaller. The economics of scholarly journals is somewhat different, but the basic culture of the journals is determined by the higher education system and by the academic profession.

It is thus universally the case that scholarly journals are integrally linked to higher education institutions. Yet, as is with books, the institutions frequently do not pay attention to their roles as sponsors and subsidizers. At times, academic policies tend to run in opposite directions. For example, while librarians facing budget cuts are eliminating subscriptions to academic journals, the editors of those journals, perhaps on the same campus, are asking for increased subsidies to make up for circulation declines. The extent of support is virtually never known, partly because the costs are scattered throughout the institution. Individual professors provide a major amount of the subsidy through their unpaid work as editors, as external reviewers, and of course as authors of articles. Academic departments and institutes, by providing office space, secretarial assistance, and sometimes postage and other expenses, are a major source of help. University presses, as publishers of journals, frequently add to institutional support. Central or faculty budgets are also important in some countries (typically in the Third World) for direct subventions for journal sponsorship.

Even in countries where the links between universities and scholarly journals are least direct, for example in socialist countries of

Eastern Europe and the Soviet Union, where journals are often published by the research institutions of the Academies of Sciences, university-based authors are prominent, and a large part of the readership is located in institutions of higher education.

Scholarly journals are part of the international knowledge network and frequently have a significant circulation outside the country of publication. The major internationally recognized journals, published almost without exception in the industrialized metropolitan nations, dominate the international journal market. Journals in nonmetropolitan languages may be influential in their own spheres and may be of very high quality, but they do not have a significant impact internationally.[25] Language is part of the equation, since most of the journals that are circulated internationally are in one of the major languages—especially English, French, or Spanish. However, several journals are multilingual, and these also play an international role. UNESCO, by publishing journals in several different language editions, helps bring scholarship from different countries, including the Third World, to an international audience.

Scholarly journals are written, edited, and produced in the major metropolitan centers and are then exported to the peripheries. Those institutions and scholars at the center have significantly better access than those at the periphery. Those outside the center—whether in Mississippi or Mongolia—are largely consumers of the scholarly journals. Universities at the periphery find it difficult to escape from what might be called the "culture of intellectual poverty" and to obtain access to either the journals themselves or even, in significant ways, to opportunities for publication in them. The cycle of poverty, so familiar in other arenas, keeps those without access to the pinnacles of scholarly prestige at a disadvantage. In this case, poverty is not necessarily a matter of a lack of financial resources. Countries like Kuwait, with considerable financial resources and a strong desire to build a top-quality university, has been unable to move into the first rank.[26] The use of a nonmetropolitan language (in this case Arabic), the lack of strong scholarly norms, inadequate laboratory and other facilities in some areas, and a number of other factors have hindered the development of the university. Thus although Kuwait University has established several scholarly journals, these journals have not moved into the forefront of international publications, although they are widely circulated in the region.

UNIVERSITIES AS GATEKEEPERS

The fact that academic institutions are key gatekeepers of knowledge is frequently forgotten and is worth discussing in the context of knowledge dissemination. Research-oriented universities create an atmosphere in which knowledge creation is valued—indeed is necessary—for promotion within the academic system. Through their presses, journals, peer review networks, academic departments and research centers, and individual faculty members, universities constitute a key validation process for knowledge. In a sense, these mechanisms decide what knowledge is legitimate and what is not. To a considerable degree, they determine what gets published and what does not. If knowledge is not certified by these academic networks, it may never see the light of day, or if it does, it may not be considered valuable.

This is an awesome responsibility, yet it is one which is seldom discussed in universities. The gatekeeping function occurs in the natural order of academic decision making and is, as one might expect, highly decentralized. Gatekeeping occurs as part of the academic personnel review process for tenure and promotion. It happens in the offices of the scholarly journals, where manuscripts, usually subjected to peer review, are accepted or rejected. And it takes place in the decisions of university presses, again aided by peer review, which determine what manuscripts will be published.

The universities, through these mechanisms of review, provide a mandatory service. Qualitative judgments need to be made because all knowledge is obviously not of equal value. The exercise of judgment is particularly important as the knowledge explosion proliferates information beyond the capacity of individuals to absorb it. Thus reliable means of making evaluations are the key to both knowledge creation and dissemination. But the fact that such a large part of the evaluation and gatekeeping function takes place in institutions of higher education is cause for some concern. Although the process is decentralized within the institution, the overarching norms and orientations of the university will tend to underlie most of the decision-making structures. Universities are conservative institutions. They are slow to change their structures, values, and orientations.[27] It may well be that the basic approach to validating knowledge is also conservative and that the gatekeepers are slow to accept innovative ideas. Antiestablishment ideas may take a long time to seep into the consciousness of the academic gatekeepers and thus achieve legitimacy. The fact that the universities hold something close to a monopoly on the validation of knowledge gives them enormous power and also special responsibilities in these matters. Decision-making structures, though decentralized, still tend to be self-perpetuating and made up of members of the same invisible colleges.[28] Gatekeepers tend to be concentrated at the most prestigious institutions, and the networks that are developed within the small circle of powerful scholars and evaluators, including journal editors and press personnel, in many disciplines is small and tight.[20]

At the international level, gatekeeping also tends to be centralized in the major institutions in the industrialized nations and tends to make it very difficult for nonmetropolitan scholars or institutions to break into the system. The network of inequalities discussed earlier is reinforced by the gatekeeping system. Even where scholars have been trained in universities in the centers, they find it difficult to remain fully up to date and linked with the network of key scholars who hold the main levers of gatekeeping power. From this perspective, while gatekeeping is decentralized within institutions, it seems highly concentrated from the outside, and access is frequently quite difficult. There is thus a curious combination of decentralization and common understandings that yield networks of gatekeepers which are not easy to manipulate. These networks may well be too conservative and bound up with not only the status and prestige systems of the major institutions, but also with established methodologies and approaches to science and scholarship.

UNIVERSITIES AS MARKETS

In many respects, universities are both producers and consumers of their "products." They hire a significant proportion of their doctorates as junior staff members. A substantial part of the pure research that is produced is aimed at an academic audience. While research funding opportunities and priorities are determined by external forces, the academic community has an important voice in determining research agendas. In this respect, academic institutions are relatively independent and play a key role in determining their own agendas and in providing a market for their graduates and their research.

Institutional priorities help to determine how funds will be spent. For example, if libraries are starved of acquisition funds, as occurred in the United States in the 1970s, the economic market for scholarly publishing changes dramatically. If universities do not purchase books and journals in significant amounts, as is true in many countries, local scholarly publishing, and by implication research, may well be curtailed. If academic libraries shift their acquisitions budgets from books to journals, as is common throughout the world, book publishers will suffer and the publishing equation shifts. In fact, scholarly publishers now can count on a smaller average sale of a scholarly book title precisely because of this shift in priorities. Journal publishers, on the other hand, are able to sell more subscriptions and to charge higher prices for their products. Universities may shift their priorities from the humanities to science and engineering, and this change will frequently affect library purchases and journal subscriptions. Subtle changes in interests and academic decisions only marginally related to knowledge dissemination can have significant implications for markets for scholarly publications.

In the United States, it is estimated that about 80 percent of the sales of university press books is to the library market—the bulk of which is to college and university libraries.[30] For scholarly journals, statistics are similar, but a larger proportion of the income comes from libraries.[31] In Europe, the market for scholarly books is somewhat more diverse, with individuals purchasing a large percentage of the output and the academic libraries in any case being a smaller network. In the Third World, the small number of academic libraries is virtually the only market for scholarly publications, since the individual scholar is frequently too poor to afford research monographs or journals. Scholarly publishing and, for that matter, the entire knowledge dissemination infrastructure would immediately collapse without the academic library market.

In the past decade, university libraries have been subjected to a variety of pressures and strains that have made them less effective "consumers" of scholarly products. Indeed, the problems of academic libraries have caused something of a crisis in scholarly publishing. Budget cuts in the 1970s were frequently allocated first to such support services as campus maintenance and the libraries. Libraries frequently cut their acquisitions back significantly.[32] The result in the United States was a major economic crisis for the university presses. As a result, there are fewer university press titles published annually now than fifteen years ago. Few new journals were added to the collections at a time when knowledge was expanding rapidly. In many libraries, journals not frequently used were dropped from the collections, sometimes breaking a run of twenty or thirty years. Staff cuts in university libraries meant that less care was taken in the selection of books and journals. All of these decisions, made for fiscal reasons, had a significant impact on the knowledge dissemination infrastructure in America.[33] As the recession of the 1970s abated and as university budgets increased, some of these pressures eased, but the fact is that the major consumer of scholarly materials is a fragile institution which can easily be damaged—with unanticipated but serious consequences for knowledge dissemination.

Data bases are another intellectual "product" which so far have been primarily linked to academic libraries. Libraries are the primary purchasers of data bases, and most users seem to work through libraries. Most libraries subsidize the use of data bases, although many are beginning to charge patrons for data base services. Private enterprise has also established data bases in specific areas, and these have frequently proved profitable. The emergence of data bases also has international implications. Virtually all the data bases are headquartered in the industrialized countries, particularly the United States. They are frequently available worldwide through the use of satellites, and users in any part of the world can join the network. But data bases in many ways reinforce the power of the industrialized powers, since those powers control the use of the bases, and a large proportion of the material in the data bases is from research in those countries.

In a basic way, since universities constitute the largest community of scholars, researchers, and students in all countries, it is not surprising that they are the major consumers of knowledge "products," from laboratory equipment to books, journals, and data bases. The academic community is also a major consumer through individual purchases by professors and students. Universities constitute communities of intellectuals who support bookstores, software markets, and other commercial enterprises which thrive because of the academic community and which contribute to knowledge dissemination. As a market for scholarly products of all kinds, the university and its environment is of primary importance in ensuring that books, journals, and other items will have a sufficient sale.

Institutions of higher education are not only teaching and research centers; they are also at the heart of the knowledge dissemination system in modern society. It is not an exaggeration to say that without academic institutions, the basic structure of knowledge dissemination would collapse. Academic institutions provide the institutional environment for the creation of knowledge through their facilities, reward structures, and ethos.[34] They also provide the major market for scholarly products. The knowledge dissemination network also has international implications in that books, journals, and increasingly data base information travel across international borders. This international network is also directly related to higher education institutions, and extends from the major centers of research and publishing in the industrialized nations of the West to much of the rest of the world.

Despite their key role in this very important enterprise, these institutions seldom have any specific policies relating to their function as knowledge disseminators. Few realize the depth or complexity of the relationship. There is little understanding of the implications of university decisions on the nature of the network. This chapter has provided a framework for understanding the complex and very important relationship between academic institutions and knowledge dissemination. An understanding of the nature of the dissemination infrastructure and the key role of universities in the network will, it is hoped, lead not only to more careful analysis of an important but unresearched area, but also to wiser policies to ensure a creative relationship between the production of knowledge and its effective dissemination.

Themes and Variations

Chapter 6

Knowledge Enigma: The Context of Copyright in the Third World

This chapter is concerned with a controversial and important part of the knowledge distribution equation—copyright. Copyright involves every aspect of the knowledge business, from the rewards that are available to an individual author and the control exercised over intellectual work to international relations among large corporations and nations with regard to the distribution of knowledge.

International copyright—the control over the international distribution of knowledge and the rules that govern the flow of printed materials across borders—is a key concern because Third World nations use knowledge from abroad and are generally dependent on foreign books. Copyright necessarily has an impact on how knowledge is distributed, on who controls it, and on the development of the publishing industry. I am concerned here largely with books, the most traditional means of knowledge distribution, and not so much with the newer nonprint means of knowledge distribution and communication, although copyright has very significant implications in those areas as well. The impact of copyright on knowledge distribution in the Third World is my main concern, along with the related theme of the relationship of textbooks to copyright in both national and international frameworks. To discuss these themes, it is necessary to consider the context of copyright in the modern world.

This is not a discussion of the legal aspects of copyright, although the bulk of the literature on copyright is, in fact, related to copyright law and its applications, both within nations and comparatively. Copyright law is a recognized specialty within legal studies, and one which is increasingly important as reinterpretations are necessary to deal with the complex issues raised by the new technologies. Although legal factors will be mentioned from time to time, my concern is with the political, economic, and intellectual implications of copyright in the context of knowledge distribution. The issues raised here have deep philosophical importance and go to the very heart of the control of knowledge, creativity, and the right of the individual over his or her work, and of course to the sometimes conflicting needs of society to have access to knowledge, whether for school textbooks or for advanced scientific research. There are no easy answers. What seems philosophically clear in one context may cause deep problems in another. Definitions are also problematical. As photocopying has become a major industry,[1] the concept of "fair use" has become a matter of considerable controversy in the industrialized nations.

THE CONCEPT OF COPYRIGHT

There are at least three basic aspects of copyright. The first stresses the moral right of the individual to his or her intellectual property and his or her essential control over that property, be it a work of art, an invention, or a book. This aspect is reflected in most of the European copyright laws and in the Berne Convention, the oldest and largest of the two major international copyright agreements. It might be summarized as copyright as a natural right or inherent moral right of the individual.[2] The second approach, nicely summarized in the United States Constitution, holds that copyright is intended to stimulate creativity and invention, and that it is a privilege that is granted to individuals for the benefit of society.[3] The American approach can be summarized as a commercial view of copyright and, in general, a way of encouraging intellectual creativity. The third approach is the societal theory exemplified by the Soviet copyright system. In this system, the society has certain basic rights over intellectual work, and the copyright laws reflect a compromise between personal rights and interests, which are recognized, and those of the collective enterprise. The concept of copyright as property, which is the key to the market economies and is basic in both the American and European approaches to copyright, is absent from the societal theory.[4]

Not everyone, of course, agrees that copyright is a good thing. One of the classic anticopyright statements is Thomas Macaulay's comment that copyright is "a tax on readers for the purpose of giving a bounty to writers."[5] Philosophical arguments have raged over the centuries concerning the nature of copyright, the justification for it, and the appropriate limits on copyright when balancing the interests of the individual and with those of society. The controversy has grown more complex in the past few decades as copyright has been applied to nonbook products such as computer programs and the like. The argument concerning regulations governing photocopies is a good example of how copyright has grown complex in recent years. The arguments revolve around rights of individuals and publishing firms on the one hand and those of the public on the other to knowledge and to the dissemination of photocopied material.[6]

Copyright stems from particular historical and socioeconomic circumstances. It emerged and gained strength in Europe as printing and distribution grew more sophisticated, industry developed, and a mass market of cultural goods become important. Literacy became widespread, and newspapers and magazines as well as books became artifacts of contemporary culture. The mode of economic organization was capitalist, and artistic creation was increasingly linked with an emerging industrial revolution and the attitudes and institutions that grew up alongside this key transformation of the nineteenth century. The role of the artist and writer that copyright protects is one based on capitalist relations and on the relationship between culture and profit. The idea of the artist and writer as a individual creator who profits from his or her work and who is engaged in a competitive enterprise with other individual creators is the key to the European and American ideologies of copyright. Thus copyright functions in a market-oriented system where intellectual goods can be bought and sold and are assigned a monetary value. Edward Ploman argues that it is surprising that copyright has gained such wide acceptance in societies with quite different economic orientations and value structures.[7] Stripped of its idealistic claims, copyright is a way of bringing the world of intellectual life into the world of contemporary commerce.

Historically, Third World nations mainly inherited the European approach to copyright, since most of the copyright laws were patterned on the colonial regulations that were in place at the time of independence. Given other development priorities, Third World countries have moved slowly to make their copyright laws indigenous.

Furthermore, there has been a good deal of controversy concerning the appropriate orientation to copyright. Current Third World thinking on copyright reflects elements of all three of the basic approaches discussed here and may, in the long run, contribute to a synthesis of theoretical perspectives on copyright and the distribution of knowledge.

The emergence of the Third World nations in the postwar era has added a dimension to the copyright concept. The issue of the creation, dissemination, and use of information in the global village has been raised largely in Third World discussions and has stimulated the controversial debates in UNESCO and elsewhere on the "New World Information Order." In these debates, issues of equity, control over the means of dissemination, and related matters are raised.[8] But virtually everyone who writes about copyright accepts the basic premises on which the concept is based—the debates are predicated on a common understanding and acceptance.

Textbooks have not been considered as a separate issue in copyright debates. It is generally assumed that schoolbooks can be treated as other publications and can be subject to the same copyright regulations as other books. In the international context, however, educational books have been recognized as beloning to a special category that should not be limited solely to commercial considerations and that should be permitted to cross borders without the same restrictions as other books. Textbooks are therefore considered somewhat exempt from rigid copyright protection because of their importance to Third World educational development.

HISTORICAL PERSPECTIVES

Although copyright has a long history, it emerged as an important idea as nations began to build up their own cultural infrastructures and felt the need to systematize and protect authors, publishers, musicians, and the panoply of new knowledge industries. Until the late nineteenth century, it was basically a national concern without international legal implications. Copyright as a world issue is of recent origin. Nations have used copyright for their own purposes for a very long period of time. The United States, as will be illustrated, was one of the world's major "pirates" until it securely developed its own cultural industry in the nineteenth century. The needs, concerns, and indeed the issues which are now of concern to the developing countries of the Third World are only very recently part of the discussion of copyright and knowledge distribution. As Edward Ploman succinctly put it:

> Copyright evolved in response to specific changes. Its origin is Western and its parentage multiple: the invention of the printing press and the advent of the Industrial Revolution, the philosophy of the marketplace, and that of natural rights, the rise of bourgeois society and the spread of literacy, new social attitudes toward art and the artist. The resulting notion of intellectual property is a European invention but is now used in diverse economic and social systems to structure the flow of information and cultural products.[9]

Historically, copyright developed in England beginning in the sixteenth century not as a means of protecting authors and intellectuals but as a means of maintaining order and discipline in the emerging book trade.[10] As England became a key center for intellectual products and for publishing, not only for its colonies but also for the United States, the evolution of copyright in England followed a rather twisted path and was informed by the concerns of the marketplace, of book publishers, and eventually of the desire of the British book trade to protect its export interests. Copyright in England was also very much linked to the laws of press control and censorship, and it functioned for more than 150 years as a means of maintaining a monopoly in the book trade. Thus, the rights of authors and artists had relatively little to do with the early development of copyright in England; such concerns emerged later and were, in some respects, stimulated by thinking in France and elsewhere in Europe. Despite this rather murky past, the Statue of Anne, which was the world's first copyright law, was passed in 1709 and did recognize the right of the author to his or her work as well as regulating the printing trade.[12]

Early copyright discussions were remarkably similar to those heard today. There was concern with how to deal with revolutionary technological developments—in this case, the printing press and its immense impact on culture and commerce. Control over copies and an effort to keep track of the result of an improved means of distribution were also topics of considerable concern in the eighteenth and nineteenth centuries. The rights of authors, on the one hand, and the control of knowledge, including censorship, on the other, entered into the equation. Finally, the rights of others involved in the business of culture, including both booksellers and publishers, were very much part of the debates. Each of these concerns has its analogy in current disucssions of copyright.

It is important to keep in mind that historically copyright developed as a national issue and had few, if any, international implications. As the book trade developed and a natural tendency for knowledge to move across national borders became evident, there were efforts to internationalize copyright, but these attempts generally failed until the late nineteenth century. Successful international efforts were pioneered in Europe, where technologies and communications developed rapidly in the mid-nineteenth century. Prior to that time, very few countries offered any protection to authors or publishers outside their borders.[13]

Nations have always used copyright for their own purposes—a fact that is easy to ignore in the idealistic rhetoric that has characterized copyright discussions in the post–World War II period. The fact is that the nations which basically control the world knowledge system—the industrialized Western powers—have convinced the rest of the world that their version of contemporary copyright is the correct and universal standard. This was not always the case. Nations have historically been most concerned with developing their own culture and publishing industries and only later have observed the niceties of copyright. Both of the world's current superpowers, the United States and the Soviet Union, were quite late in joining the international copyright system. Imperial Russia did not strictly adhere to copyright rules, and the revolutionary Soviet regime followed that tradition, only joining the international copyright community in 1974.[14] The American attitude toward copyright is, in many ways, a classic example of how copyright has been flouted—and used—in the process of developing an independent literature, culture, and publishing infrastructure.

The United States in the nineteenth century was very much a developing country and looked to Europe for cultural and intellectual cues.[15] The first American copyright act, passed in 1790, specifically permitted pirating of foreign published works.[16] The general thrust of the 1790 act was that copyright is a privilege and not a right and therefore could be significantly restricted. The American printing and publishing industry grew up around the ability to freely print foreign works and sell them in the United States without obtaining permission from the overseas authors and without paying any royalties. Some of America's best-known publishers developed by imaginatively obtaining copies of popular works of fiction in England and quickly printing them in the United States. Charles Dickens, among many other British authors, frequently complained about his economic losses due to American "pirating." In many ways, America's printing and publishing industries benefited significantly from a system that depended on freedom to publish without payment the unprotected works of foreign authors.[17] It is also significant that even when the United States began to offer copyright protection to foreign authors and began, slowly, to participate in international copyright activities, it retained in its copyright law a "manufacturing clause" that demanded that books by American authors be printed in the United States in order to have American copyright protection. This clause was the subject of considerable controversy in the debate concerning the 1968 copyright revision and is at the present time under discussion in the United States Congress.[18]

The first significant American participation in international copyright was in 1891. The United States did not formally participate in any of the established international copyright conventions until the Universal Copyright Convention (UCC) was established in 1952—and the UCC was in fact set up largely to bring the United States and most Latin American countries which followed the American lead into the fold of international treaties. In some respects, the unwillingness of the United States to offer protection to foreign authors until quite late helped build up an independent American publishing and printing industry.[19] In others, it retarded the growth of American authorship and made it difficult for Americans to earn a living by writing, since publishers could easily publish foreign (mostly British) authors without paying royalties. It is quite clear that the United States used copyright for its own purposes and that, from the European point of view in the nineteenth century, the Americans were the worst pirates in the world.

THE INTERNATIONAL COPYRIGHT SYSTEM

International copyright protection is a recent development, and it too resulted from the growth of technologies, of the increasingly international use of such languages as English, French, German, and Spanish, and of the emergence of international centers of book publishing and scholarship.[20] Prior to the nineteenth century, international protection of copyright was rare, and it was possible only through an increasingly complex web of bilateral treaties. By the mid-nineteenth century, the web of copyright treaties in Europe was sufficiently confusing that an international conference was called that resulted in the International Convention for the Protection of Literary and Artistic Works, popularly known as the Berne Convention, in 1886.[21] It is the oldest copyright treaty in the world and has gone through several revisions, the most recent of which directly concerned Third World nations and aroused a good deal of controversy. As of 1979, there were seventy-one states in the Berne Convention, with the notable exceptions of the United States, China, and the Soviet Union.[22] The Berne Convention is administered by the World Intellectual Property Organization (WIPO), which helps to solve disputes, provides interpretations, and keeps records and statistics. It reflects the Western European concept of copyright and was developed to protect interests of the European nations as publishing and printing became major industries as a result of the industrial revolution and the rise of mass literacy and public education. The national copyright laws of the European powers were altered to place them into conformity with the requirements of the Berne Convention.

It is beyond the scope of this chapter to discuss in detail the Berne Convention. Its basic commitment is to protect the rights of individual authors, and its philosophical orientation is toward the natural right approach to copyright. The treaty set a minimum standard of copyright protection that was then binding on all of the signatories. Countries can provide more protection than stipulated by Berne, but they cannot offer less. In 1948, a revision of the convention gave it even stronger precedence over national copyright regulations. The Berne Convention requires its participants to conform in considerable detail to its rules, and it has been generally successful in obtaining this conformity. One of the interesting aspects of the Berne Convention is that a work (written, artistic, or other) has protection from its date of creation whether or not it is formally registered officially with a national copyright office. This protection is offered only to the signatories of the convention. The length of copyright protection, an issue of considerable controversy in copyright debates, has been gradually extended so that it is now the author's lifetime plus fifty years.

The second major international copyright treaty was established under the auspices of UNESCO in 1952, and is currently administered by UNESCO.[23] The Universal Copyright Convention (UCC) was developed largely as a means of bringing the United States and a number of Latin American nations into the international copyright system. It was, simply stated, a compromise between the Berne Convention and the United States view on copyright.[24] American copyright law traditionally has offered significantly less protection to copyright holders than European rules, and the UCC similarly is less inclusive than the Berne Convention, although both treaties provide basic rights of copyright, and many countries are members of both the Berne Convention and the UCC. The UCC sees copyright in a larger context that includes issues such as the development of literature and the dissemination of knowledge. As a result, factors other than the simple protection of rights of authors enter into the equation. Unlike the Berne Convention, which stipulates that all original works have basic copyright protection regardless of whether they are formally registered, the UCC permits nations to have registration procedures and spells them out. The UCC also offers a shorter term of copyright protection—twenty-five years.

CURRENT ISSUES AND COMPULSORY LICENSING

The copyright agencies and international organizations like UNESCO, as well as the major publishing nations, have pressed for the widest possible adherence to the copyright system, and they have been quite successful in convincing many Third World nations to draft or strengthen their own national copyright legislation and to join one or more of the international treaties. There has also been some pressure from the Third World countries on the copyright agencies to make it easier for those countries to obtain rights to translate or reprint books from abroad, and they have had some success in this area.[25] In addition, there is constant litigation and debate concerning the scope and meaning of copyright, the definition of 'fair use' in the age of the photocopying revolution, and the appropriate limits to copyright protection in the face of pressures for equity in the international system. The copyright agencies have sponsored a number of full-scale conferences on copyright revision and have in fact made some substantive changes in copyright. The basic theory, structure, and politics of international copyright have remained basically stable since the establishment of the Berne Convention in 1886 and the inception of the Universal Copyright Convention in 1952.

It is useful to highlight this discussion of change in the international copyright situation by referring to one of the most heated debates on international copyright in the postwar period, the Stockholm conference of 1967 and the follow-up Paris meetings in 1971, where Third World nations demanded significant alterations in the copyright system to protect their interests. They stressed a loosening of copyright protection in the interest of equity in knowledge distribution and as a means of permitting relatively speedy reprinting and translation of books related to education and scientific development. The end result was a compromise. As one observer put it: "The major publishing nations recognized the needs of the developing countries for inexpensive textbooks and measures that would enable them to publish such editions. But they regarded the proposals of Stockholm as too drastic and refused to go along with them. The conflict endangered the very existence of the international copyright system."[26]

The Third World countries were attempting to loosen copyright protection for books in the field of education and science by introducing a mechanism of compulsory licensing that would permit Third World publishers to reprint or translate material after a period of time since original publication had elapsed and after efforts had been made to contact the original publisher and obtain permission to reprint, without necessarily having that permission in hand.[27] They were also forcing a debate about the meaning of copyright in the context of North-South inequalities and in the face of domination of the copyright system by the major industrial nations. The discussions at Stockholm were heated and resulted in an agreement which provided significantly liberalized rules for the Third World nations. This agreement proved to be quite controversial. In fact, Britain refused to go along, and other major Western publishing nations expressed reservations. After further protracted discussions and another conference under UNESCO auspices in Paris in 1971 which included representatives of both the Berne Convention and the UCC, a solution was found which provided some liberalization but which also prevented books obtained under compulsory licensing procedures from being used for commercial profit, and a commitment that such books should not be exported from the country of publication.[28]

While it is now possible under established procedures for Third World nations to obtain compulsory licenses to reprint or translate text and educational books, there are still significant limitations that reflect compromises between the industrialized book-producing nations and the Third World consuming countries. For example, it generally takes at least three years for a compulsory license to be available for publication in English, French, or Spanish. Those in less universal languages require only one year. Each license is issued only for the country in which it is to be used, and the books are not supposed to be exported.[29] Thus Third World interests were, in the end, successful in establishing the basic concept that there must be some flexibility in the international copyright system to recognize the inequalities between nations and the particular needs of the Third World countries. But the major copyright powers were also successful in limiting the scope of the reforms and in binding the Third World to the international copyright system. They were able to limit the reforms to educational books and books used for advanced scientific purposes. General books, fiction, magazines, and the like are not subject to compulsory licensing at the present time.

While there were serious debates about the basic nature of the copyright system prior to the reforms, virtually everyone is now committed to the system and is willing to work within it for reform. Those countries which are currently outside the international copyright system, such as China and Malaysia, are moving, albeit slowly, to join. Copyright is a curious amalgam of ideology, belief, and pragmatism, but those responsible for the growth and development of copyright, first as a national and later as an international instrument, have been pragmatic.[30] Copyright, with few exceptions, protects the "haves"; it is a form of monopoly that gives basic control over knowledge to the creator of that knowledge or the designee (usually a publisher, or these days, a software company).[31] Indeed, it was developed more than three centuries ago in England precisely to protect monopolistic practices.[32] Copyright has also been used for censorship and in its early days was seen by the authorities as a means of controlling knowledge.

THE CONTEXT OF INEQUALITY

Copyright functions in an interdependent international system of intellectual and related commercial relations among nations. I am concerned here with the specific problems of the Third World in developing indigenous culture and educational systems and the infrastructures that go along with them. The fact is that the nations of the Third World find themselves at a considerable disadvantage when building their own knowledge systems in this network of inequality. Copyright is but a small part of a much larger international system that relates to the control over resources, trade, foreign assistance, and many other factors. Yet, by looking at copyright as a microcosm of the larger system, it is possible to see in some detail the nature of the disadvantages faced by the Third World.

The international network of knowledge distribution is one of considerable complexity. Book publishers, film distribution enterprises, news networks, and recently data bases and computer firms are all part of the system by which knowledge is distributed throughout the world.[33] Academic and scientific institutions play a role not only in the creation of knowledge, but also in its distribution. Individual scholars and intellectuals are themselves very much a part of the system.

The fact of inequality is clear. The bulk of the world's scientific research is done in a few of the industrialized nations—notably the United States, Britain, Japan, France, West Germany, and the Soviet Union. It has been estimated that close to one-quarter of the world's expenditures for research and development are spent in the United States. The major universities, with their well-equipped libraries and laboratories, are located in a handful of industrialized nations. These institutions attract the best scholars, and, incidentally, train a significant portion of the highly educated personnel from the Third World.[34] By every measure, the bulk of the world's productivity in terms of research and scientific development is largely in the industrialized nations.[35] This fact has many implications. The research needs of the industrialized nations are naturally those served by this research, and the channels of dissemination are geared to the producing nations. Most of the markets for scholarly books and periodicals are in the industrialized nations, and this fact further skews the knowledge dissemination network. The largest academic libraries are located in the industrialized nations and constitute the main source for the purchase of scientific books and journals. A large academic profession (as well as student population) are a further source of both the production and consumption of intellectual material.

Language is a key factor in the international knowledge network .[36] English is the first language of 345 million people and the second language of another 400 million, and it is the native language of twelve nations and the semiofficial tongue of another thirty-three countries.[37] This fact gives English a considerable advantage as a language of scholarly communication and research. Along with Spanish, French, and, to a lesser extent, Russian, English dominates the knowledge distribution network. A large majority of the world's major scholarly journals and many academic books, the key means of knowledge distribution, are in English, and most of the rest are in the other three major international languages. Even in Europe, scholars in countries such as the Netherlands, Sweden, and even West Germany frequently publish their work in English to achieve the maximum international exposure.

Third World countries are dominted by the major international languages, and this dominance places a further strain on limited publishing and other resources. It also makes these countries dependent on the nations which publish in the major international languages. The necessity to translate material from English (and to a lesser extent from the other international languages) into a variety of Third World languages creates problems relating to the technical expertise to do the translations, the ability to publish those translated works, and the need to function in the framework of the international copyright system in order to secure permission to do the translations in the first place. The need to translate material was one of the basic issues that stimulated the demand by Third World nations to ease the process of obtaining permission to reprint and translate materials. It must be remembered that the vast bulk of the world's translations are made from the major international languages into a variety of smaller and less powerful languages (in this instance, including large but scientifically less-developed languages like Chinese, Hindi, Bengali, and Portugese, among others). The business of knowledge transfer is largely carried on in the currency of the major international languages, and the nations using these languages—and publishing in them—have a considerable advantage.

The infrastructures of knowledge dissemination are basicaly controlled by the industrialized nations. The prominent publishing firms are located in those nations, and those firms control the production and to a major extent the distribution of books around the world.[38] There is a large trade in the export of books from the industrialized nations to the Third World. The major publishers have branches throughout the Third World and are, in fact, multinational enterprises. Indeed, about half of the sales of the British publishing industry are dependent on overseas trade, much of it to the Third World. The French have a similar interest in book exports, while the Americans, with only 10 percent of their publishing export related, are somewhat more insular; nevertheless, they too have had a growing interest in export sales, for political and cultural reasons as much as for commercial motives. Book exports and the impact of books from the industrialized nations on the Third World are not only matters of profit, but are also directly linked to the foreign policy goals of the major industrialized nations.[39] It is therefore very much in the interest of the major book-exporting nations to continue their role as centers of the knowledge creation and distribution system.

Not only do the physical means of book creation and distribution—the publishers—exist in the industrialized nations, but the decision-making apparatus for books and scientific and educational knowledge in general are in those countries. The major journals are edited from a few nations—largely the United States, Britain, and, for the francophone world, France. These countries constitute the major intellectual centers, and much of the rest of the world is in a peripheral relationship to them. The decisions made by journal editors, book publishers, and others who are gatekeepers of knowledge reflect the intellectual and scientific environment in which they function.

While the basic technologies of book production, typesetting and printing, are widely disseminated throughout the world—and in fact several Third World nations, including India, Singapore, and Hong Kong, do a significant amount of printing and typesetting for publishers in the industrialized nations, sometimes with the latest technologies—the basic technological innovations and developments occur in the industrialized nations and are, in general, controlled by them. Third World nations must import, often under license, these new technologies, or they must purchase machinery abroad. All of this continues a situation of dependency on the industrialized nations. Even such a basic element of book production as paper, the technology for which is simple and widely disseminated, is basically controlled by a few industrialized nations, with the consequence that prices tend to be high.[40]

The impact of the very newest technologies will be considerable on the Third World, and the development and control of these innovations are also located in the industrialized nations. Data bases are located in the West and are tied into the major international languages and use material generated from Western sources. Satellite communications systems are similarly centralized in terms of international communications, although several Third World nations, including Indonesia and India, have their own satellites which are used for educational and other purposes. The hardware for the new technologies, such as the newest reprographic machines, is manufactured in the industrialized nations and are usually quite expensive, as well as difficult to repair. This situation, too, creates problems for Third World nations.

The point of these comments is that the network of knowledge creation and dissemination is both complex and unequal. The copyright system is very much a part of this system of interrelationships. In part, the sheer weight of market forces, the major language of publication, the location of the basic infrastructures, and the nationality of most scientists and authors dictate that the industrialized nations, and particularly the major publishing nations such as the United States, the Soviet Union, Britain, and France, are the major centers for knowledge creation and distribution. The structure of the international network also plays a role. The multinational publishers are well established, and their vested interest in maintaining the status quo is considerable. Finally, the policies of the industrialized nations in many instances serve to protect the status quo because it is frequently in the interest of those nations to maintain control over the structures of knowledge dissemination.[41] It is hardly surprising that copyright should be enmeshed in this powerful system and that those who are peripheral to this complex and powerful international system, the developing nations of the Third World, should wish to extricate themselves from it.

THE ISSUE OF PIRACY

Piracy is big business. It is estimated that $1 billion worth of books and another $1 billion of tapes and cassettes are pirated annually.[42]

These alarming statistics do not include unauthorized photocopying, which is also a major problem for copyright holders. Piracy is usually defined as the unauthorized publication of a book, tape, cassette, or, recently, computer software for commercial sale. Piracy takes place in all countries, but it has become a key issue among publishers as it relates to the Third World because the bulk of the world's large-scale commercial piracy is done in the Third World. The publishers of the industrialized nations are very disturbed about piracy and have applied pressure not only on Third World pirates, but also on their own governments in an effort to link, for example, favorable foreign trade terms or economic aid to the eradication of piracy. In some cases, this effort has been effective. For example, the government of Singapore is currently revising its copyright law and stepping up enforcement in response to pressure from the United States, Singapore's largest trading partner. Book piracy has its ups and downs in the major pirating nations (currently located mainly in South and East Asia), but the practice continues, largely for economic reasons. Taiwan, for example, has been probably the largest book pirate and still engages in the practice, but the scope of the piracy has declined significantly. This decline is due to external pressure, but perhaps more importantly to the growing sophistication of the Taiwan economy, which makes it in the national interest to respect copyright, patents, and the other legal regulations of the transfer of knowledge and technology.[43]

What is piracy and literary theft from the point of view of the industrialized nations is something else to Third World publishers. While few in the Third World are currently willing to publicly support violating the international copyright laws, there are some arguments to be made against copyright regulations in general and as they apply to the Third World in particular. There is, of course, a line of argument in opposition to the concept of copyright which claims, among other things, that a system that creates a monopoly and limits access of knowledge on the basis of who originally produced the knowledge is unfair and unwise.[44] And as one Third World spokesman put it: "We in Southeast Asia and the Third World are the countrysides of the urban-industrial publishing centers of the West. And just as with most countryside populations, we are perennially treated to avowals of concern for our development from the metropolitan powers—to no avail."[45] There is a clear difference of opinion concerning piracy, although at the present time few openly espouse violation of copyright rules. What is not discussed, however, is done on a large scale in many countries. As one Western publisher stated, a large number of countries (including a few industrialized nations) are known as pirates. In 1980, the following were among the nations mentioned as significant violators of copyright: Taiwan, Korea, and the Philippines (as the three largest pirates), Singapore, Peru, the Dominican Republic, China, Pakistan, Hong Kong, Malaysia, Thailand, Indonesia, and Egypt. Countries in which piracy occurs only on an occasional basis include West Germany, the Netherlands, Syria, India, Colombia, Japan, Iran, Iraq, and a few others.[46]

Book piracy occurs in many different ways. In a few countries, such as Taiwan, unauthorized reprinting of books from abroad is a significant part of the publishing business. Taiwan pirates specialize in producing English-language book titles and selling them in the East and Southeast Asian region and occasionally in the West. Popular trade books, reference books (including the *Encyclopaedia Britannica*), key medical books, university-level texts, and many others in editions looking exactly like the original but generally printed on poorer-quality paper are widely sold at prices of well under half the original cost of the book.[47] Publishers, or frequently free-lance printers, reprint a few titles which they think can be sold quickly. These books are frequently best-sellers from the West which have a brisk sale in many Third World nations. These same publishers and printers also produce school or college textbooks, which can be easily distributed with little financial risk. Much piracy seems to be the relatively unplanned efforts of those in the book business who wish to make a quick profit or satisfy an immediate local need.

There is also the business of unauthorized translations from Western languages. Either through lack of effort or because negotiations with Western publishers break down or costs are too high, many Third World publishers fail to obtain formal permission to publish translations of Western works. There are no statistics on the issues of unauthorized translations, but the volume must be fairly significant. The titles involved are of all kinds, but frequently educational books are involved because there is a ready market for translations of school and college textbooks and the Western publishers of such books are sometimes the least informed concerning the needs of the Third World book industry. Indeed, the call by Third World nations for compulsory licenses stemmed from this dilemma, and the campaign proved to be most successful with regard to school and college textbooks.

A recent development in piracy, stimulated by the rapid growth of technology and the increasing sophistication of a number of Third World nations, relates to the unauthorized reproduction of computer programs, software of all kinds, and, increasingly, microcomputers and computer parts. These items are generally protected by copyright laws. A mini-industry related to computer technology has developed in such countries as Singapore, Taiwan, and Hong Kong. The pirating of tape cassettes and phonograph records has long been a problem in Southeast and East Asia.

It can be argued, on the one hand, that pirated books in question rob the original publisher (and of course the author) of their fair share of royalties and prevent the author from controlling when and where his or her work should be published. On the other hand, the editions brought out in the Third World constitute a very minor share of the world market for most books: the profits earned by the original publishers from such editions or from export sales to those countries would be a tiny fraction of the total. It can also be argued that the pirate is frequently creating a market for the book, since an imported version would be too costly for the local book buyers. Third World publishers have frequently complained that Western publishers are slow to respond to requests for reprint rights, that they charge too much, or that they are uninterested, preferring to export a small number of copies at high prices rather than granting rights for a larger, low-cost, edition. It is often said that American publishers are not sufficiently attuned to the export market to be able to effectively handle that business, and that the British publishers, dependent on that market, prefer to export their own books rather than grant rights.

The issue for textbooks and scientific books is somewhat different, since in general mass markets are not involved. Third World book people have argued that the West already dominates knowledge creation and should not be able to prevent knowledge distribution. Books used for educational purposes, therefore, should be freely reprinted or translated in the Third World without undue delays from complex negotiations with Western publishers or the payment of high fees. It is also pointed out that many Third World nations lack foreign exchange to pay for book imports or reprint rights and that this is another reason for an open market for reprinting books, particularly for educational purposes. The discussions of compulsory licensing revolved mainly around the need for educational books in the Third World. It is probably the case, although statistics do not exist, that since the liberalization of the rules for compulsory licenses, the amount of unauthorized reprinting or translating of educational and scientific books has diminished significantly, although it is likely that pirating of popular books and reference books continues in a number of countries. The Western publishers have been engaged in a major campaign to eliminate book piracy, and while there has not been complete success, there has been a definite increase in copyright consciousness in the Third World.

It is also the case that what is piracy to one nation is fair use to another. The People's Republic of China does not now belong to any of the international copyright agreements and thus is not bound by them. China, however, is currently in the process of drafting a copyright law and will join one of the international copyright treaties. The Chinese engage in extensive translations of books from the major Western languages (and from Japanese) and publish them without paying any royalties or obtaining permission. Such actions are not illegal under current Chinese law. A number of other Third World nations have enacted far-reaching compulsory licensing laws which permit them to use foreign published materials fairly freely. Publishers in industrialized nations claim that this is piracy, but under local laws it is not. While it is likely that book piracy is on the decline as a result of liberalized copyright rules and a greater spirit of compliance in the Third World, the phenomenon of computer-based piracy is no doubt on the increase.

TECHNOLOGY AND COPYRIGHT

Copyright is not only faced with its traditional problems of obtaining compliance from a variety of different countries, of dealing with divergent philosophical perspectives, and of aligning many different national legal perspectives, but it must also deal with one of the most important challenges in a long period—the impact of contemporary technology. For the Third World, the new communications technologies hold both promise and problems, but it can be argued that the problems outweigh the promise. It is not possible to discuss all of the technological challenges facing the dissemination of knowledge here, but it is useful to focus on those aspects of the technological revolution that directly affect copyright and that have special implications for the Third World.[48]

The new technologies, such as data bases, new computer-assisted composition and printing techniques, and the rapidly developing field of reprography, are all developing in the context of the global inequalities which were described earlier. While Third World nations may be able to make use of some of these innovations, they originated in the industrialized nations and are, with few exceptions, produced in them and controlled by interests in the North. The Third World is a consumer of the new technologies, generally on terms set by the industrialized nations. The innovations are frequently but not always expensive, and they are inevitably "high tech", meaning that Third World nations do not have the infrastructure to manufacture these items and frequently have problems in assimilating them into the existing technologies. While one commentator recently argued that the new technologies will permit the developing nations to "leap-frog" the traditional technologies and move directly into the twenty-first century, a more realistic assessment is that the new technologies are a continuation of the pattern of inequality and continue to place the Third World in a position of dependency on the industrialized nations—even exacerbating the situation in some ways by introducing very complex and expensive technologies that are difficult to assimilate.[49]

Virtually all the new technologies have implications for Third World knowledge distribution and for copyright.[50] The development of data bases, for example, has the potential for bringing the latest knowledge from worldwide sources to the Third World, but it also will inevitably tie users to the major international language of Western knowledge dissemination (English), to the hardware provided by the corporations which have developed and own the data bases, to the conceptions of knowledge and research which are used by the owners, and to the high costs of obtaining material through the data bases. This technology will also strengthen the split between the urban centers in the Third World, which are more likely to have access to these new technologies, and the rural peripheries, which will not. The copyright system means that the collectors and disseminators of data base knowledge will have basic control over it. Thus the Third World nations will be consumers of knowledge created and distributed by Western sources in the English language. The fact is that large parts of the Third World will simply be cut off from data base knowledge systems altogether because of the cost or because the local infrastructures are inadequate to absorb and use the new technologies.

Technological innovations in printing and composition also have mixed, though generally more positive, implications for the Third World. Although these developments are products of Western technology and are for the most part manufactured in the industrialized nations, they give Third World nations with small-scale publishing industries the possibility of building up their local capability at relatively low cost. New innovations in computer-assisted text composition do not require extraordinarily expensive technology. For Third World nations, such as India, with establish "low tech" publishing industries, these trends are a mixed blessing, although India has been able to use new composing technology to produce texts for export. For countries, such as Malaysia, which are building up a publishing industry, these new technologies are potentially very valuable. Computer-assisted photocomposition of text material has stimulated small-scale publishing and has lowered the cost of producing short-run publications and books in the West. This technology can also help the Third World, where printings for scholarly and educational materials may be small.

Photocomposition, a widely used printing innovation, has also been a boon to pirating and to reprinting material in general. This fact, of course, has major implications for copyright because it reduces the cost, and therefore the economic risks, of piracy. It is unlikely that the Taiwanese printers would have been so active in reprinting Western books if the technology for quickly reproducing material without setting it into type did not exist.

One of the most significant technological challenges to copyright is the photocopying revolution—a revolution which continues to improve ways of quickly, inexpensively, and expertly photocopying printed material of all kinds. In the United States, photocopying of published material now runs into the billions of pages annually, and a significant part of this photocopying takes place in clear violation of the copyright laws. The concept of 'fair use', included in the new American copyright law, is being constantly defined in the courts, but nevertheless is ignored by most individual copiers and by many institutional users as well.[51] The intricate, yet very important, issues involved in issues such as the photocopying of journals of dissemination in library-based networks are beyond the scope of this essay, but as the Williams and Wilkens case in the United States indicates, this topic goes to the heart of the survival of academic journals (one of the key means of knowledge distribution), the role of libraries, and the implications of dissemination networks in a technological age.[52] In a number of countries, copyright authorities and the courts have been trying to accommodate copyright protection to the rapidly advancing technologies of reprography, thus far with only modest success.[53] Technological developments have far outstripped the capabilities of the copyright system, either within nations or internationally, to adequately control the situation. Some have argued that authors and publishers would survive without strict controls over copying and that, in fact, reprography contributes more to society by giving easier access to knowledge than it takes away by limiting the economic benefits to knowledge producers.[54]

In many ways, photocopying has been a boon to Third World nations. The basic technology of reprography is not very complex, and machines are produced in some Third World nations, or they are imported. While there are no adequate data, it seems that there are fewer controls on the use of photocopying and that knowledge users have easier access to photocopied materials than in many industrialized nations. It is possible, for example, to obtain photocopied and bound copies of books in a number of Third World nations at prices well under those of the original publication. This easy access may reduce the cost of imported books but may have other implications for the knowledge distribution system. While the industrialized nations have struggled with ways to control photocopying through legal restrictions and other means, Third World nations have not as yet dealt with the implication of the advances in photocopying technology.

It is probably true that the past several decades have brought more technological change to knowledge production and dissemination than has been the case for a very long time. These innovations in communications, printing, and copying have come at the same time that many Third World countries have been trying to build up a basic knowledge industry.[55] The possibilities of using the new technologies to develop an efficient and cost-effective knowledge industry are considerable and have been used by several countries—mainly those with highly trained personnel to use the new technologies, such as Singapore and Hong Kong, which have become major printing and publishing centers. Other Third World nations have combined old technologies with elements of the new. But many nations have found that entering the new age of knowledge production has been very difficult, and have remained dependent on outside agencies, usually the Western-based multinational publishers, for their book needs, often including school textbooks.

The international system that tries to control knowledge dissemination—copyright—has struggled to keep up with the new technologies as well as with the other challenges that have been discussed in this essay, and the result has been considerable confusion. The basic protections provided to authors and publishers under the copyright agreements are difficult to interpret in the light of some of the technological innovations and even more tricky to enforce.

TEXTBOOKS AND COPYRIGHT

The production and distribution of textbooks for schools and post-secondary education is an important but specialized part of the total knowledge distribution process. In the Third World, textbooks constitute the dominant segment of the publishing enterprise. In some smaller developing countries, textbooks are virtually the only indigenous books published. In many nations, as already discussed, textbook publishing permits other kinds of publishing to occur because it provides the economic base for the industry. Even where primary-level text publishing is in government hands, which is increasingly common in the Third World, upper-level text and educational publishing is a mainstay of publishing. In the United States, textbook publishing is the largest single segment of the publishing business, accounting for 30 percent of the income of American publishers.

Textbooks are not only a key element in the publishing industry, but are also crucial for a nation's educational system. Without adequate textbooks, the effectiveness of the school is hampered. Some research has argued that texts are among the most important elements in ensuring success for students.[56] Most nations have recognized that textbooks must meet the educational needs of school pupils and that they should reflect national values and orientations. In this respect, Third World countries face special problems, since a number of small countries still import schoolbooks, frequently from the former colonial power.

Decisions concerning who should produce and distribute textbooks is also a key Third World issue. Textbooks were frequently imported during the colonial period and after independence were published by local affiliates of multinational publishers (or imported). The traditional production and distribution facilities continued to be used—perhaps to the detriment of the emergence of an indigenous publishing industry. Later, many Third World governments moved to nationalize schoolbook publishing by establishing governmental agencies which had responsibility for writing, editing, producing, and distributing school texts. While this arrangement did produce indigenous books, it also created problems. Very frequently, the efficiency of these operations was low and the costs tended to be high. Furthermore, when the most lucrative and steady part of the publishing business was removed from the private sector, independent publishers found it very difficult to build a business by tapping only the general and library markets in their countries.[57] Thus, unanticipated consequences of the nationalization of the textbook business included the weakening of the local indigenous publishing industry and unnecessarily high production costs for school texts.

Copyright plays an important role in Third World textbook publishing. The international aspects of copyright are relevant, since many books or segments of books include imported materials. National copyright regulations are also important because they govern the publication of all books within a country. On the international level, the provisions of the Berne Convention and the Universal Copyright Convention cover all books, including texts and educational books. Thus, educational publishers are covered by the same restrictions that affect publishers generally. The one important exception to the broader copyright coverage is compulsory licensing, which permits Third World publishers and educational agencies to more easily gain access to books and journals published in the industrialized nations. The specific regulations governing compulsory licensing are complex and do not permit completely free access to overseas material, but the arrangement, which is now part of the international copyright system, permits easier access and also in some instances reduces the cost of using foreign materials for educational purposes.

Many Third World textbooks are adapted, in whole or in part, from educational materials developed in the industrialized countries. The legal copyright protections afforded to such adapted material is less clear than for other material. The copyright treaties deal with the broader questions of appropriate quotations from copyrighted works, but freely adapting material is not covered. Furthermore, national copyright laws vary on these issues, and it is sometimes difficult to understand the ramifications of the legal restrictions. It is the case that there is widespread adapting—and sometimes simple reproduction of materials—in Third World textbooks because the pressure to publish textbooks is intense and there is frequently a dearth of qualified local writers and curriculum experts. It is particularly common for textbooks published in some of the less widely used Third World languages to freely adapt or copy foreign materials without regard to copyright restrictions. The legal, as well as the moral, political, and educational, consequences of such adapting and reproduction are issues which have not been fully addressed by many involved in textbook development and publication.

National copyright regulations also have a considerable impact on textbook development. Textbooks are subject to national copyright laws like other books, and exceptions to copyright regulations are not found in those laws. Third World copyright regulations stem largely from the laws put into place by the colonial powers or are borrowed from the major Western copyright laws. Thus, there is no special Third World approach to copyright, and the laws found in the Third World resemble one of the three major ideological currents in thinking about copyright. Few Third World nations have modified their copyright laws to reflect the specific needs of their specific national circumstances. Textbook developed must therefore fit into the context of national laws, which were patterned on foreign models.

Textbooks publishers must be aware of the copyright rules relating to their work. Legal restrictions on the use of copyrighted materials such as illustrations in books, on the length and use of quotations, on the length of copyright protection, and on translation rights must all be kept in mind by textbook authors and publishers. In general, national copyright laws do not provide any specific rights to educational publishers or educational books. Copyright laws protect authors and publishers and make the use of copyrighted materials subject to the interests of the copyright holders. It is usually possible for textbook publishers to observe national copyright laws and still publish good textbooks. Of course, such compliance may add to the cost of textbook development because copyright holders may require payment for permission to use or adapt material. Copyright also adds a layer of bureaucratic procedure as well, since materials can only be used with appropriate permission.

Third World textbook development is handled in many different ways. Where a ministry of education is responsible for text development and publication, it is often possible to easily surmount copyright problems, since much of the needed local educational material is very likely in the hands of other government agencies. Where the private sector is involved, restrictions may be greater. In most Third World countries, copyright problems stem more from the need to adapt and use foreign materials than with national copyright regulations.

Third World textbook publishers have had to weigh the advantages and disadvantages of reprinting, translating, producing locally written texts (which are frequently based on curricular models and materials from foreign material), or importing books. Copyright considerations enter into this equation in a significant way, since the flow of knowledge is controlled by the international copyright system. The roles of multinational publishers, of ministry of education officials, of the private-sector publishers in the Third World, and frequently of school officials are important. Both purely economic and cost-related issues and questions related to educational and social policy enter into the equation concerning decisions about textbook production. Copyright is very much part of the situation as well. It is an aspect which frequently delays textbook production and means that textbook authors and planners must modify their educationally generated plans to meet commercial and legal mandates.

THE FUTURE OF COPYRIGHT IN AN UNEQUAL WORLD

Copyright is well entrenched and powerful as an idea and as a set of legal mechanisms for controlling the international flow of knowledge.[58] There seems to be a powerful international consensus, including most Third World nations, in favor of the basic international copyright system as it has developed since the late nineteenth century and particularly since it has been modified since World War II. The adherence of the United States in the nineteenth century and of the Soviet Union in the mid-twentieth century (after both nations flouted copyright as they built their own national publishing industries) means that all of the world's major publishing nations, except for the People's Republic of China, are part of the system. After considerable controversy during the 1960s, the industrialized nations have provided some of the modifications that Third World nations demanded and a workable compromise seems to have been struck.

The problems facing copyright, however, are quite formidable and can be summarized as follows.

1. *Technological.* The adaptation of the concept of copyright and of the international copyright system to reprography, unauthorized use of copyrighted materials due to photocopying, and data bases are perhaps the most difficult basic problems facing copyright now and in the coming decades.
2. *Legal.* The drafting and implementation, at the national and international levels, of codes to regulate the copyright system in the face of these new challenges is considerable.
3. *Control.* An issue frequently ignored but one which is particularly important in the context of Third World concerns is the basic question of who controls knowledge and what these controls mean. Copyright, in many respects, works to the advantage of the "haves" over the "have-nots" in terms of knowledge. At the present time, most Third World nations have decided not to pursue this question, preferring to work in the context of the copyright system as it exists and recognizing that the control over the flow of knowledge rests with the industrial countries.
4. *Size.* Knowledge is expanding at an ever-increasing rate. Indeed, the new technologies permit the production, dissemination, and bibliographic control over knowledge to expand. Both the expansion of knowledge and the new means of disseminating it creates problems for copyright.
5. *Equity.* In the light of the North-South debate over knowledge control and access, the heated debates of the 1960s concerning Third World access to knowledge in all of its forms are a continuing issue. While dormant at the present time, this inequality is nevertheless an underlying contradiction in the international copyright system.

It can be argued that critics of the contemporary arrangement of knowledge control and flow made their major thrust in the 1960s by applying pressure on the international copyright system and also through agencies like UNESCO, where calls for a "New World Information Order" were heard.[59] The debates within the international copyright system and the departure of the United States and Britain from UNESCO seem to have silenced the critics, at least for the present.

There is an international consensus, regardless of political ideology, economic organization, or position in the knowledge hierarchy, that anarchy in knowledge creation and distribution is to be avoided. For the present, most agree that the international copyright system, despite its inequalities, provides the best means of controlling the situation, especially in the light of massive technological change. Whether the significant internal contradictions in the copyright system will stimulate dissent and questioning at some future time is not clear. Despite the stresses, some piracy, and the lukewarm adherence of some Third World nations, the international copyright system appears to be accepted as the basic structure to regulate the international flow of knowledge.

Chapter 7

Textbooks in the Third World

Nothing has ever replaced the printed word as a key element in the educational process, and, as a result, textbooks are central to schooling at all levels. Yet textbooks are seldom taken into account by those who plan educational reforms or expansion of school systems. Textbooks are particularly important in the Third World, not only because educational expansion has been especially impressive but because new subjects have been introduced into the curriculum requiring new texts. Further, in situations where there is a shortage of teachers and where teacher training is sometimes limited in scope, textbooks are crucial in maintaining standards of quality and direction to the curriculum. In a recent study, Heyneman et al. noted:

> From the evidence we have so far, the availability of books appears to be the single most consistently positive school factor in predicting academic achievement. In fifteen of the eighteen statistics, it is positive; this is, for example, more favorable than the thirteen out of twenty-four recently reported for teacher training.[1]

The creation, production, and distribution of textbooks is a complex process involving many parts of a society's infrastructure. The publishing industry is involved, as are the educational establishment, writers, and, inevitably, government departments. In the Third World context, international agencies are often involved as well—international organizations, multinational publishing corporations, and the like. The copyright laws often intrude into the text business. Good textbooks require planning, development, funding, testing, and distribution.

Textbooks utilize substantial quantities of paper and require printing facilities. They are the product of the coordination of educational, governmental, publishing, and printing resources.

The purpose of this discussion is to analyse the broader context of textbook creation and distribution in the Third World context. While publishing and the textbook business are not major financial expenditures in the broader context of educational and economic development, they none the less involve many elements of a modern society. The interrelationships are important to understand if the need for textbooks is to be effectively met.[2] It is necessary to examine the history of textbook development, contemporary international implications, the relationship between the text market and general and scholarly publishing, the role of the public and private sectors in the textbook enterprise, and, of course, the articulation between textbooks and the educational system.

There are many varieties of textbooks, and each has a different relationship to the educational system and to publishing generally. By far the largest segment of the text market produces books for primary and secondary education. With the worldwide expansion of education in the past several decades, the need for textbooks has dramatically increased. In addition to quantitative growth, the curriculum has become more complex, necessitating specific books in new fields of study. In many Third World nations, for example, basic texts concerning the history and culture of the country are lacking, and must be created for the schools, as well as for general use. Textbooks for post-secondary education are also needed. In many Third World nations, university-level texts have traditionally been imported and often do not reflect indigenous needs. The problems of post-secondary texts are quite different from those of school-level books. Finally, books for new literates are not, in the traditional sense, textbooks, but they are none the less directly related to the needs of the educational system, and articulation between texts and the materials needed to maintain literacy is very important in societies with high levels of illiteracy.[3]

The keys to effective textbook development are not massive fiscal expenditures or crash programs, but rather careful coordination, attention to the articulation between the educational system and the publishing industry, linking of curricular development and expansion of enrollments to textbook requirements, and involvement of the necessary expertise in the development of relevant and high-quality textbooks. The textbook situation in any country depends on the state of the publishing industry (including printing capacity, the availability of paper, and the distribution network), the presence of competent authors (and the research and testing facilities to ensure relevant textbooks), and the educational system.

THE HISTORICAL CONTEXT

Historical factors are important in understanding contemporary educational realities in the Third World. The heritage of colonialism in much of the Third World determined the structure of educational systems, the language of schooling, and many aspects of the curriculum. Links to metropolitan centers were imposed during the colonial period and in many cases remain to the present. Multinational publishers, for example, often with their headquarters in the former colonial home country, retain considerable influence in the Third World.[4] Third World nations have attempted to break with colonial traditions, but strong influences remain in many nations.

Textbooks, during the colonial period, reflected the curricular orientations of the colonizers and were often written by colonial officials and published in the metropolitan country. Even when textbooks were published in the colony, they were based on foreign models and reflected the orientations and policies of the colonial authorities. Educational policies reflected the needs of the colonial authorities, and curricula reflected these orientations.[5] The basic fact of colonialism is that key decisions in education were made by others, who had priorities far from the difficult processes of nation building and economic development.

With almost no exceptions, Third World nations entered the post–World War II period lacking the basic infrastructures of publishing. In many cases, textbooks were imported from the metropolitan country. In others, branches of metropolitan publishers were responsible for textbook production. Indigenous publishers were rare, and educational authorities had little expertise in textbook production and distribution. All the requirements of a modern publishing system—printing facilities, a distribution apparatus, competent editors, and the like—had to be developed. In this direct sense, the heritage of colonialism was one of dependency on a foreign country.

The curriculum was also patterned on colonial practices, and change was slow. Foreigners had not only directed the educational system, but had determined the meaning of politics and culture. As a result, both the curriculum and many of the textbooks inherited from the colonial period were outmoded. Examples from the metropolitan country abounded in the curriculum, and new conceptions of history, national development, and priorities had to be devised. Then the educational system had to adjust to these priorities and develop curricula, and textbooks, to suit these needs. Education was, in most cases, limited to a small urban elite, and literacy was limited to a small segment of the population. The language of education was, in many instances, exclusively the metropolitan language. Every newly independent nation strove to expand educational opportunities and foster literacy. Thus, the problems of creating textbooks not only for a new curriculum, but for educational systems undergoing simultaneous rapid expansion, were substantial.

Colonialism had contributed to an international system which emphasized the power of the metropolitan centers and the relationship between these centers and the various peripheries. The organization of the publishing enterprise reflected this unequal distribution of intellectual resources. Basic decisions concerning publishing and, for the most part, the publishing apparatus itself, remained in the metropolitan country. Trade relationships emphasized this arrangement.

Even in those parts of the world which were not under direct colonial rule, such as Thailand, China, most of Latin America, and even Japan, the influence of European educational patterns, ideologies, and emphases was very strong. Such countries had a substantial degree of formal autonomy, but they were deeply influenced from abroad. European experts were prominent in educational and curricular planning, and the organizational patterns of education reflected European models almost without exception. Noncolonized Third World nations were more able to produce their own textbooks and were less dependent on foreign models for the curriculum, but they too were very much linked to an international system of inequality in education.

Historical factors continue to weigh heavily. The educational policies, language priorities, and curricular orientations of the colonial period still influence many Third World nations. The cost of recreating an educational system has been great and has placed special burdens on textbooks, since they are often the first representation of the new educational reality. The historical organization of the text business, with an emphasis on foreign experts, foreign printing capacity, and foreign technology, has been difficult to break. The multinational publishers retain considerable influence in many Third World nations, particularly where a European language remains important in education. Historical traditions and policies must be kept in mind in any consideration of textbook development in the contemporary period. It is easy to demand a break with the past; it is much more difficult to implement truly independent policies and practices.

THE INTERNATIONAL CONTEXT

Neither textbooks nor educational systems in the Third World exist in a vacuum. Partly as a result of historical traditions, which have been discussed, and partly because of contemporary realities, textbook production and distribution are involved in an international system of publishing and knowledge distribution. This international system is largely dominated by the industrial nations and often used by them to maintain dominance. The elements of the system range from international copyright arrangements, the location of multinational publishing companies, and their impact on markets in the Third World, to the control of new printing technologies, the world price of paper, and other factors. The policies of the industrialized nations concerning educational affairs, publishing, and related matters also relate to the nature of textbooks in the Third World.

Textbook production has often been in the hands of publishing firms located in the industrialized nations. These firms, multinational in nature, continue to be very important in the textbook business. Macmillan, Longmans, McGraw-Hill, Prentice-Hall, and others are household names in many nations. Even such prestigious firms as Oxford University Press are deeply involved in the production and distribution of school-level textbooks in many nations. The trend is away from the domination of the text market by multinational firms, but their influence remains strong.[6] In Zimbabwe, for example, most textbooks have been produced by Longmans or Macmillan, which have a well-developed presence in the country. The multinational firms have a number of distinct advantages over indigenous publishers.[7] They are often able to produce books for more than one country and can market them regionally. This is the case in both English-speaking and French-speaking Africa, where the national markets are small and regional distribution is not too difficult. Here the large firms can purchase paper on international markets at low cost and can allocate resources, such as paper, among their regional offices. The multinational firms have access to the most modern technologies and can introduce them, as needed, in their Third World affiliates. Perhaps most important, the multinationals have ready access to cash, a constant problem among Third World publishers, can invest needed sums in textbook development, can utilize modern printing techniques, and can print in large numbers, thereby reducing unit costs. The multinationals have all the expertise necessary to engage in sophisticated and effective publishing. They are able to do research and development for textbooks to ensure that the final result is of high quality.

The multinationals have some distinct disadvantages for the Third World as well. They are concerned basically with the welfare of the corporation and not primarily of the country, and their publishing decisions are made with their own interests in mind. Textbooks produced by the multinationals may or may not be directly relevant for particular Third World nations. Such books are often designed with a regional market in mind and typically retain a strong element of the perspective of the metropolitan publishers. They are frequently edited and printed in Europe or North America, and consequently local publishers obtain no benefit from these books. The publishing infrastructure of the consuming nation is not strengthened as a result of these books. The technical quality of the textbooks is generally quite high, and they often include pictures and are printed on good-quality paper. This has both advantages and disadvantages. On the one hand, the books meet international production standards. On the other, they may be expensive and unnecessarily elaborate for the local market. These books, because of their marketing advantages, quality, and large printings, often make the emergence of indigenous textbooks very difficult. Without question, the multinational publishers have a good deal of influence in the international textbook configuration. They set the standard for texts and are able, in some markets, to continue to dominate the production and sales of textbooks. The multinationals, in recent years, have begun to publish in Third World languages, and they have thereby spread their influence. Branches of multinational publishers in such countries as Zimbabwe, Nigeria, India, Malaysia, and many others are actively producing books in local languages for specific markets.

In a sense, the contemporary concept of the textbook is a Western idea, and most Third World nations depend on notions of textbook design, production, and appearance initiated in the industrialized nations. The idea that texts should have full-color illustrations, be printed on long-lasting paper, be accompanied by workbooks printed on newsprint, and that they should generally be hardbound rather than paperbound, are all Western concepts. Many Third World nations attempt to follow these ideas about text design without major alterations. In some countries, paperbound books printed on cheaper paper are used in order to reduce costs or because of the lack of quality paper. In a few instances, books are specifically designed to meet local needs rather than to conform to international standards. Clearly, the Western concept of the textbook may need alteration in the Third World context.

The international copyright system has some implications for textbooks and is symbolic of the international knowledge system. The international copyright arrangements are dominated by the industrialized nations, and Third World nations have attempted with some success, through UNESCO and other agencies, to gain more control over the system.[8] It is sometimes difficult for Third World publishers to obtain permission from copyright holders to reprint or translate materials. The bureaucratic procedures involved are complex and time-consuming. The copyright issue is more important with university-level textbooks, where there is often a need to translate or reprint materials from the industrialized nations. Publishers in these nations sometimes prefer to sell their own books (at high prices) rather than to grant licenses for local printings. At the school level, copyright issues are not generally a key concern, but the entire question is symbolic of the nature of the international knowledge system.

New ideas and technologies typically emanate from the industrialized nations and are important for the advancement of the Third World. These innovations are dominated by the industrialized nations, and Third World countries must try to obtain access to them through the international system. Computer-assisted typesetting, new techniques in graphic design, and printing technologies that utilize fast and efficient presses have all been pioneered in the industrialized nations. Expensive equipment must often be purchased. Trained personnel are not generally available to make efficient use of these new technologies. Yet, in the long run, textbooks can be produced more cheaply and with better quality by using the new technologies. They also permit the industrialized nations to have a significant technological advantage in the international marketplace of ideas, and to be able to market textbooks internationally which are both attractive and inexpensive.

A final element of the international equation is the specific governmental foreign-assistance policies of the industrialized nations. Some have argued that these policies are detrimental to the interests of the Third World.[9] In some cases, foreign aid programs have assisted textbook producton and distribution. The British government has provided English-language college-level textbooks to many Third World countries. Such books, while useful to students, contribute nothing to the development of local publishing industries and do not help build capabilities for indigenous textbook development. Similar efforts have been sponsored by the United States, the Soviet Union, and the Federal Republic of Germany. Franklin Book Programs, a private American foundation that received funding from the United States government and other sources, assisted the development of textbook capabilities in a number of Third World nations. UNESCO has also been concerned with textbook production and distribution. Some of these programs have assisted the development of local textbook capabilities, while others have provided imported books.

Although textbooks, particularly at the primary level, seem like purely local matters, it is clear that there is an important international dimension to the textbook equation in the Third World. There is, of course, a great deal that Third World nations can learn from the technologies and experiences of the industrialized nations. There are also areas in which international agencies and perhaps individual industrialized nations can constructively assist the Third World. But the negative implications of the international system must also be kept in mind. Such matters as the restrictions of international copyright, the complex roles of the multinational publishers, and even the mixed results of foreign-aid programs must be carefully considered.

LANGUAGE

The issue of language has implications far beyond textbooks. The choice of medium of instruction in the schools and in higher education has broad educational and often political importance. Conflict over language is evident in many Third World nations. In numerous countries, educational systems are in the process of shifting the medium of instruction from the colonial language to one or more indigenous languages. Such language shifts, along with the expansion of education and an increasing diversity of curricular offerings, have placed great pressure on textbook development. In many countries, indigenous languages have not previously been used for modern schooling, and appropriate vocabularies have to be devised before textbooks can be written. Even where languages have a long educational tradition, new subjects necessitate the "modernization" of the language. Thus, language has both policy implications and related technical problems for textbook development. Once a decision is made to use a particular medium of instruction, the complex process of textbook development begins.

The following language-related issues have implications for the development of textbooks.

Vocabulary. Appropriate vocabularies for specific subjects included in the curriculum must often be devised before textbooks can be written.

Spelling. In some languages, there is no commonly agreed-upon spelling for many words, particularly in the emerging fields that must have textbooks.

Typefaces. It is often necessary to devise new typefaces to meet the needs of languages not previously used for educational purposes.

Printing capability. This is a broader problem, but printing capability in indigenous languages may be even scarcer than facilities in the metropolitan languages.

Translation. It is often necessary, at least at the initial stages, to translate textbooks from metropolitan languages into indigenous languages. Problems of copyright, quality of translations, relevance, vocabularies, and other matters make this a difficult task.

Some Third World nations have several languages which are used for educational purposes. In India, at least fifteen languages are in widespread use for education. In such situations, the problems of textbook development become even more complicated. The National Book Trust in India as well as several private-sector publishers have attempted to produce textbooks in a number of languages that utilize common design, graphic, and pictorial material. These texts are simultaneously translated into different languages. This has resulted in a number of economies.

Third World nations have increasingly adopted one or more indigenous languages for educational purposes, and this has placed additional strains on their capacity to produce textbooks. The broader political and educational issues involved with language choice and use are key issues, as are the detailed and often mundane aspects of implementing language policies in the textbook field.

TEXTBOOKS AND PUBLISHING

The relationship between textbooks and the publishing industry in the Third World is complex. There has been an increasing trend for government agencies to take a direct role in textbook production and distribution, in the interest of producing books more cheaply and ensuring that they meet requirements of the educational system. This tendency has had both positive and negative implications. The publishing industry, often in private hands, has been deprived of its largest and most lucrative market, and this has constrained the development of the industry. Governments have found that textbook production is a more expensive and complicated process than envisaged, and delays have occurred as costs have risen. The development of a fully fledged publishing infrastructure solely for textbooks has been a formidable and costly process. In some cases, however, direct government involvement has ensured that texts meet established standards and are inexpensive, even though they are often subsidized.

As decisions are made concerning the location of textbook publishing, it must be kept in mind that in the Third World textbooks are the largest segment of book publishing and therefore crucial to the health of the book enterprise as a whole. Even where publishers are to some extent not confined to one country, as is the case in several African nations, textbooks may still be an economically important part of their work. Textbook publication must be seen as part of a larger publishing enterprise. In many countries, without at least part of the textbook market, other less profitable aspects of publishing cannot thrive.

The textbook process may be divided into three distinct phases: development, publication, and distribution. In the United States and most other market-economy industrialized nations, all three phases are in the hands of private-sector publishers who undertake to meet the requirements of school authorities at the national, state, or local levels. Public authorities generally approve specific books or sets of books and then purchase them from the publishers for distribution (usually without cost) to the schools. The publishers have established divisions devoted to textbooks, and are able to develop appropriate books by paying authors, test-marketing materials, editing, and then designing the books. Many publishers have entire sets of books aimed at specific grade levels or subject areas. The books articulate with various aspects of the established curriculum. When school authorities implement changes in the curriculum, the textbook publishers move quickly to provide books to serve the new developments. In many countries, there are a number of competing sets of textbooks issued by different publishers, thus providing school authorities with different alternatives in terms of design, approach, and sometimes philosophy. In the industrialized socialist societies, textbook publishing is generally done by government agencies in collaboration with education authorities. Again, there are elaborate infrastructures to assist in textbook development and production.

In many Third World countries, the development and publication of textbooks is not clearly defined. In some countries, the private sector, often multinational publishers, has responsibility for textbooks. In others, government agencies produce some books while private publishers produce others. Typically, post-secondary texts are in private hands while school-level books are a responsibility of the government. In yet other nations, government agencies have full responsibility for textbooks. Textbook production is characterized by a good deal of confusion, overlapping of authority, and frequent changes in policy.

An effective textbook policy must not only provide the required books to the schools, but must also take into account the capabilities and needs of the entire publishing infrastructure. Government takeover of textbook production has, in some countries, made it very difficult for private-sector publishers, who have responsibility for publishing cultural books, fiction, and often research studies, to survive. The text market traditionally made it possible for them to engage in less profitable publishing ventures. Thus a government decision has implications beyond the text situation itself. By leaving textbook production in the hands of the private sector, the state is indirectly subsidizing these publishers to do other kinds of publishing.

Educational and government authorities are often unaware of the complexities of the textbook business. Costs rise very quickly when the requirements of maintaining editorial staff, designers, and, in some cases, printing facilities are added. Government agencies are seldom able to keep costs low in their textbook efforts. Even in the industrialized nations, government printing enterprises are often more costly than those in the private sector, because of higher labor costs and lack of familiarity with the nuances of publishing.

There are, of course, some advantages to government involvement in the production of textbooks. Greater control is possible over both content and design, and the costing of books can be more exactly determined. It is often assumed that textbooks can be more quickly produced by specialized agencies than by general publishers, and this is sometimes, but not always, the case.

There clearly are trade-offs involved in decisions concerning who should publish textbooks and how such publishing should be financed. These basic decisions are in the hands of governments and educational authorities, and the publishing industry responds to them. Basic decisions have widespread implications. Removing the text market from the private sector can severely hamper the ability of Third World publishers to issue general and scholarly books and to develop technical expertise. The availability of printing facilities, expertise in design and editing, and other factors are also crucial to basic decisions concerning the location of the textbook publishing apparatus. Fiscal decisions concerning subsidies of textbooks are also pivotal, since such decisions determine the cost of books, the economic possibilities of private-sector publishing, and related issues.

INFRASTRUCTURES

Publishing textbooks is by no means a simple matter. Textbook development and publication are an integral part of both the educational system and the publishing apparatus. In order to produce textbooks successfully, there must be a range of skills and physical facilities available and working in coordination. The following elements constitute the key parts of the 'textbook infrastructure'.

On one side, the educational system must be capable of designing curricula and successfully integrating teaching materials (of which textbooks are perhaps the most important, but by no means the only, aspect). Once basic policy decisions have been made regarding the subjects to be taught, the basic philosophy and approach to teaching, and the detailed content of courses and grade levels, it is then possible to transform these decisions into appropriate learning materials. Without question, the basic curricular decisions are key decisions and require an approach to the psychology of learning and the sociology of the school population, in addition to decisions on course content. Many nations have curriculum development agencies that have responsibility for developing curriculua and often for working on appropriate texts and other learning materials.

In order to design effective textbooks, content must be clearly presented at an appropriate grade level. This task requires the cooperation of writers adept at presenting materials in an interesting way, and specialists in learning theory and cognitive development who can ensure that the content is presented in a manner that is pedagogically effective. Sociologists must ensure that text material relates to societal realities and is relevant to students. Textbooks designed for specific grade levels must be articulated with other levels, and related subjects coordinated as well. In many Third World nations, basic curricular materials must be designed in an original format to meet the particular needs of the society. Models used in other countries may be useful, but countries in need of instilling a sense of national unity are generally quite careful in designing appropriate text materials for courses on history and in related fields. Even language books are necessarily related to issues of national development and integration.

The range of educational expertise required for textbook development is considerable, and the cost of producing effective text materials is often high. For many Third World nations, the requisite range of expertise is not available and the quality of material suffers. Where nontext supplementary material is needed, as is increasingly the case, costs increase and the amount and scope of necessary expertise grows. For example, simple audio-visual materials require their own infrastructures for design and use in the schools.

While basic textbooks are the main concern of this discussion—and of most educational planners in the Third World—there are related needs that must be met as well. Supplementary printed materials, such as workbooks, teachers' guides, and consumable items such as standardized tests, are directly related to textbook development. Audio-visual materials, where these are relevant and practical, must be coordinated with the basic curriculum and with texts. Nontext neo-educational books are also crucial in the Third World. For example a range of reading materials for new literates is crucial if the gains that have been made in literacy are to be maintained. Studies have shown that such materials are needed to maintain literacy over time. Reading material for new literates is not generally a responsibility of textbook publishers, and it is an item often neglected by educational officials. Such books can be produced by the private sector—a good example of this is the famous 'Onitsha Market books' of Nigeria—or by other agencies. The point here is that planners must take into account the range of educational materials needed by a population undergoing education at a number of levels.

The publishing infrastructure is just as complex and in some respects more capital intensive in the sense that it requires not only expertise, but also an expensive physical plant for the production of modern printed materials and the infrastructures necessary to distribute these materials. The skills required in publishing are specialized and often in short supply in the Third World. Careful editing is a key element in the production of any book—including a textbook.[10] Editors must have a detailed knowledge of the language in which they are working, as well as a "feel" for the elements of a book. Editing is a specialized skill that comes with experience. The editing of textbooks is a subspecialty which requires additional expertise concerning the nature and needs of educational systems and some knowledge of learning theory. Textbook editors typically work more closely with authors, and often have a greater hand in the actual writing of a book than is the case for general book editors.[11]

Publishing also involves book design and coordination of the various aspects of the production process. Such technical matters as the choice of paper, the style of type, the specific kind of printing technology, and of course the number of copies printed all affect the quality and the price of books. Textbook publishing is somewhat specialized in that durability and price are generally more important than innovative artistic design. In addition, in textbooks, educational purposes and the traditional factors of book design must be effectively meshed.

Decisions concerning the type of paper, the use of color pictures, and the binding all affect the price, durability, and attractiveness of textbooks. The provision of information concerning these often complex decisions involves a great deal of technical competence, and the publisher is prepared to provide this expertise.

It is obvious that textbooks require printing presses, paper supplies, and ancillary machinery such as binders. Many Third World countries lack at least some of these basic components. Paper is a particularly difficult problem, since a paper industry is very costly to build and requires raw materials which some countries do not possess. Paper, when purchased on the international market, is often quite expensive. Further, Third World paper industries do not often produce the variety of papers desirable for textbooks. Printing facilities exist in almost every country, but advanced technologies which permit large and inexpensive press runs are often lacking. Computer-assisted typography is rare in the Third World, and in some countries binding is still done primarily by hand. The lack of advanced technologies limits flexibility in text design and production.

The distribution of textbooks is not as difficult a problem as the distribution of general books, since in most cases school authorities are responsible for getting books from publishers to students. Nevertheless, in a few Third World nations transportation facilities are rudimentary, and the lack of a basic system for book sales and distribution hinders easy dissemination of texts.

The infrastructure of the book industry, in human as well as material terms, affects the production and distribution of textbooks. In most Third World nations, one or more of the elements of a modern book industry is missing, and this creates difficulties and delays and often results in a lower standard of published material. As educational authorities and publishers attempt to design texts and relate books to supplementary curricular materials, the availability of the infrastructures required to produce needed materials must be kept in mind.

ARTICULATION

The coordination of materials, agencies, and expertise is a key element in textbook development. The articulation between the educational system and the publishing apparatus (whether a government publisher or the private sector) is particularly crucial and often is neglected in the overall planning of textbooks. A good textbook requires a long period of gestation. Once basic educational decisions have been made, a difficult enough process in itself, the design and preparation of a textbook is time-consuming and requires a range of expertise. Ancillary materials need to be coordinated with the textbooks, and all of these activities require organization. Text materials need to be pretested and then the books designed, with attention paid to both educational and publishing factors.

In many countries, the publisher is the overall coordinator of the text enterprise. In others, and especially in the Third World, education ministries have responsibility for the articulation of the effort. As a combination of intellectual effort and the integration of printing and other services, the development of textbooks requires careful coordination at all levels. This is often a neglected aspect of the enterprise, and the lack of articulation and coordination results in inefficiencies and increased costs. It is important to have one agency responsible for the entire process of textbook development, so that the process functions in a unitary, integrated fashion. Those responsible for coordination should also have the necessary technical expertise to understand the various parts of the complex process of textbook development.

Textbooks are an integral part of the educational enterprise and are especially important in the Third World. Because of variations in the quality and training of teachers, regional differences, and a lack of clearly understood educational approaches, the textbook is at the heart of schooling. It, in a sense, provides the cement for the school system and is an essential link between those who determine the curriculum and the student in the classroom. Good texts cannot ensure quality education, but they can provide a minimum of uniformity. In countries with a large number of newly literate people, textbooks and quasi-text materials aimed at the populations of 'new literates' are fundamental. In order to maintain literacy, it is necessary to have access to books. These books need to be aimed directly at this population and articulated with literacy efforts.

The process of text development and production is a complex one in any nation, and particularly difficult in the Third World. Infrastructures are often weak and the demands on skilled manpower great. The relationship between basic curricular and other educational decisions, the publishing enterprise, and the distribution apparatus is close and often neglected. Third World nations must understand not only the importance of textbooks as a part of education, but also the technical aspects of textbook development and production. There exists a variety of mechanisms for producing textbooks, but the key element is an understanding of the totality of the effort and an appreciation of its complexity.

Chapter 8

The Role and Nurturing of Journals in the Third World

Despite the spread of computer-based technological innovations and data bases, journals remain the most important means of disseminating knowledge worldwide. Precisely because of their relatively simple technology, they have played a crucial role in the Third World, and will continue to do so for years to come. This chapter will discuss the broader function of scholarly journals, the implications of the international knowledge system for journals in the Third World, and some of the options for more effective development and distribution of scholarly journals there.

Journals have significant advantages as a means of international scholarly communication. They are relatively inexpensive. They use technologies which are available to virtually every nation and to most academic institutions, regardless of age or level of development. Through a well-established international infrastructure of library acquisition, new journals can reach concerned scholarly audiences fairly efficiently. Finally, as the traditional means of communicating knowledge internationally, journals are accepted and recognized by scholars and researchers. As noted in previous chapters, journals define what is important, maintain standards, and also help to create an "invisible college" of those concerned with a topic. Not infrequently, the invisible college unites around the journal.

They are, moreover, more than a means of communication. Journals report new knowledge; they interpret research; they provide a forum for debate and discussion. In a sense, they define the nature of their field and what is legitimate knowledge within that field. A journal that is innovative and aware of new trends can help push forward the frontiers of knowledge. One that has a particular bias can harm the development of a field or at least hinder the emergence of new and perhaps innovative orientations. Indeed, a journal can help to establish the legitimacy of a new field of study as well as help to define it, and may be founded by a scholarly association in part for this reason. An example is the *Journal of Popular Culture*, which played a key role in developing the study of its subject and which has a much larger role than the Popular Culture Association which established it. The *Comparative Education Review*, established in 1955, similarly helped to legitimate the study of comparative education and stimulate research in the field. Thus, journals are of particular importance in developing new fields of study. They can also provide a voice for new or perhaps dissident approaches in an established field of study. The *Bulletin of Concerned Asian Scholars*, for example, provided a voice in the United States for scholars who were opposed to the war in Vietnam during the 1960s and helped to legitimate radical approaches to analysis of Asian research.

The role of journals in developing fields of study and concern is of special importance in the context of the Third World, where many areas of study are relatively new or at least not covered in the established scholarly journals of the industrialized nations. Journals can also provide for Third World scholars an immediate means of communicating with scholars in other countries and with the major centers of research in the industrialized nations. For this they do not require large circulations. A scientific field may be small in terms of the number of scholars or users of its knowledge, but it may be important nevertheless, and the journals which it sponsors may be quite influential.

THE INTERNATIONAL KNOWLEDGE NETWORK AND ITS IMPACT ON JOURNALS

Journals do not exist in a vacuum. The international context of scholarly publication has major implications for the nature of journals, for their authors, and for the economics and politics of knowledge distribution.[1] This international context is particularly important for journals operating in Third World nations because their domestic markets are frequently too small to ensure a successful publication.[2] The fact is that most of the world's production of knowledge, and an equally large proportion of its distribution, takes place in the larger industrialized nations. The great majority of prestigious and influential scholarly journals are published in industrialized nations and are circulated internationally. As a result, the language of scholarly communication is generally that of the major industrialized nations—usually English or French, occasionally Spanish, German, or Russian. The widespread use of English, particularly, gives those scientific communities and journals using it as a medium of communication an immediate advantage and much easier access to the international knowledge network and to the results of research and development.[3]

The basic infrastructures for the distribution of knowledge are located in a relatively few industrialized nations. The United States, Britain, France, and West Germany constitute the major knowledge producing nations. (The Soviet Union is also a major producer but does not play as much of an international role, in part because of the difficulty of obtaining access to Russian-language materials, in part because of the extent to which Soviet science is shrouded in secrecy.) The major academic and scientific library systems—major markets for scholarly publications—are also located in the industrialized nations. It is, of course, much easier to create a new journal if there is a ready library market easily accessible. It is much easier as well to obtain relevant editorial and technical expertise in the industrialized nations. Most of the major book publishers are in the North, and a number of these publishers issue journals as part of their publishing program. Elsevier, a Dutch publisher, alone issues about two hundred different scientific journals, most of them in English.

The fact that most of the journals are edited and published from the industrialized nations has major implications for the Third World. The most important internationally circulated journals tend naturally to cater largely to readers located in the industrialized nations and not to the small minority of their readers in the Third World. Indeed, the Western journals generally pay relatively little attention to Third World needs. They use scholarly and methodological paradigms that are related to the major Western academic systems. The debates in their pages are Western debates. The scholarship reported, in general, is Western scholarship based on Western concerns and using Western data. There is little prejudice against Third World scholars. There is simply little consciousness of the issues facing scholars outside the industrialized nations.

In fairness, it must be added that editors in the West face practical problems in dealing with potential authors in the Third World. The time it takes to communicate with them is a problem—and in some countries the postal system is unreliable as well as slow. It is also difficult to involve Third World scholars in the all-important peer-evaluation system of the major international journals. Those journals' external reviewers generally come from the industrialized nations, and almost exclusively from the country in which a journal is published or its near neighbors. This means that, however international in consciousness a reviewer might be, the concerns of Western academic systems are paramount in the evaluation process. Editors also recognize that for financial reasons only a small portion of their readers will live outside the industrialized nations. Journal prices normally reflect the costs of production and the economics of the country of publication.[4] As a result, the prices of Western scholarly journals are often extraordinarily high in the Third World—out of reach of virtually all individual scholars and even difficult for libraries.

In short, the majority of scholarly journals are published in the industrialized nations, and the knowledge network is essentially controlled there. Scholars work within this unequal set of relationships and assume that they are part of the natural order of things. Thus, many Third World scholars prefer to publish in international journals rather than local publications, even when these exist. They assume that articles in the international journals will receive wider circulation and might be noticed abroad—perhaps resulting in invitations to seminars. Third World academic institutions frequently foster this sense of inferiority by giving international journals more weight in decisions concerning promotions. The frequently inadequate infrastructures of Third World journals also make many scholars hesitant to contribute to them, since there are often delays in publication. The *West African Journal of Education,* for example, the major publication in its field on the African continent, is now several years behind schedule.

It is easy to implore Third World authors to publish in domestic journals and common to hear Third World scholars excoriated for their lack of national loyalty for publishing abroad. But under the circumstances it is not surprising that international journals are generally the first choice. This means, of course, that Third World scholars must orient their writings to the interests of the international journals, even if these concerns are not particularly relevant to their own countries. They may also write in English or French rather than their local language because of the possibility of exposure to an international scholarly audience. These are the ways they have learned they must follow in order to participate in the international knowledge network.

CONTEMPORARY JOURNALS: PROBLEMS AND PROSPECTS

Libraries everywhere in the world are unable to keep up with the postwar proliferation of journals, and this situation is growing worse in the face of continuing austerity in acquisition budgets. The greater number of journals also makes it difficult for individual scholars to keep up with new knowledge in their fields. The retrieval of research has become of paramount importance. For libraries and scholars in the Third World, these matters are particularly pressing. Subscriptions are costly, hard currency scarce, and, even when these conditions are met, physical delivery through the mails uncertain. Efficient abstracting and bibliographic services, frequently computer-based, are generally unavailable, and are in any case expensive.

Two editorial trends have been noticeable in scholarly journals. One is to become more specialized, serving a more limited group of scholars. My own field of education, for example, has produced journals devoted solely to fields such as higher education, comparative education, and cognitive educational psychology. At the same time, interdisciplinary journals have emerged to cross traditional academic boundaries—or, in some cases, to create new specializations. Some of the older, more general journals are having problems in maintaining an identity in fields of study which have dramatically changed and in maintaining their circulations in the face of more specialized publications more directly aimed at the newer research communities. Third World scholars may have difficulty understanding how to fit into this new set of scholarly relationships, how to achieve for their journals international acceptance, or even to know which journals are available in the West for their scholarly output.

The issue of language has already been mentioned. In scholarly journals circulated internationally, the use of English has increased dramatically in the past twenty years. Even countries such as the Netherlands, Sweden, and West Germany, which have active and well-established intellectual lives of their own, have followed this trend in some journals, since English-language publications have immediate access to the largest and more prestigious markets and thus attract the largest numbers of potential authors.

Some Third World nations have consciously chosen to use their own national languages as the major media for scholarship and higher education. Malaysia is one of these countries, and its successes and failures are illustrative. On the one hand, several Malaysian scholarly journals appear in the national language, Bahasa Malaysia, and attract contributors and readers in Malaysia. But there remains an overwhelming dependence on scholarship produced in the industrialized nations, and Malaysian scholars are still keen to have their work published in English abroad. Indeed, the Malaysian universities perpetuate this situation by encouraging their academic staff to publish abroad and by stressing such publication for promotion. In most fields, the major scholarly contributions appear in English, although there is increasing respect for and acceptance of scholarly publication in the local language. India, on the other hand, has generally used English as the major means of national communication. So far there has been very little research on the impact of the language of scholarship on national academic development. The issue, however, is one of crucial importance for the development of study and research in the Third World—not to speak of the non-English-speaking scholarly communities in the industrialized world as well.

It is also important to consider the key role and nature of editors in the development of scholarly journals. Again, there has been little analysis in the literature on scholarly communication. The editor is the most important person in deciding what gets published and what does not.[5] If an editor is aware of current trends in a field and highly motivated, the journal will likely be lively and useful. If the editor is not paying much attention to the journal or is behind the times, the journal will be less interesting and useful. Editors may approach their tasks with preconceived ideas or ideological or methodological biases, or they can do their best to exercise unbiased judgements. There are, of course, many kinds of editors, but it is possible to make a few generalizations. Most editors of journals in the industrialized nations are scholars of some seniority and prominence in their fields who are willing to dedicate time, energy, and discipline to the task. Most serve without remuneration. Most are published scholars themselves. Few devote their full time to their journals and many have other responsibilities, most frequently teaching but often administrative. Seldom are they selected with any view to international interests, contacts, or consciousness, and thus it is only by happenstance that some journals have an international orientation. Indeed, the pressures against international orientation are considerable. Correspondence is slow and time-consuming. Few editors, particularly in North America, have the linguistic ability to deal with materials in languages other than English. Funds are rarely available to translate manuscripts from one language into another. One of the few agencies with a commitment to translate and publish material in a variety of languages is UNESCO.

While scholarly editors in the industrialized nations seldom have any formal training for the position, they have often previously served on editorial boards and have been involved in the appraisal process as reviewers. They are part of a culture of scholarly journals, and can learn about the nature of editing from people, perhaps on their own campuses, who have had such responsibilities. They are usually in office long enough, generally at least five years, to develop reasonable expertise.[6]

In the Third World, on the other hand, a comparable infrastructure is frequently missing. Editors cannot turn to the same range of expertise for help. Sometimes basics, such as efficient secretarial services, are unavailable. Perhaps most important, the culture of objective evaluation of manuscripts, of asking for revisions and perhaps of rejecting the work of colleagues, may not be as well entrenched. Working as an editor in many Third World contexts may be more a matter of establishing norms and cultural values relating to a scholarly journal than of maintaining a tradition that is well established and accepted by the academic community. Conditions obviously vary from country to country, but pressures of many kinds are often evident. Universities or other agencies which have established a journal may wish to retain some control over it. Editorial independence may be difficult to maintain. Often there is a dearth of publishable manuscripts, particularly in academic systems in which a premium is placed on publishing abroad, or in which there is not great pressure to publish scholarly materials. The role of the editor is significantly more difficult and complicated in the Third World than in the industrialized nations.

THIRD WORLD CHALLENGES

There are many reasons why the establishment and nurturing of scholarly journals is important to the Third World.[7] Its scholars, for reasons indicated earlier, cannot rely on the international (Western-oriented) journals to publish their work; they can look more optimistically to local journals which may be more oriented to their interests. Indigenous journals can also focus attention on the issues, problems, and approaches that are most relevant to their own regions or countries. More fundamentally, journals are a key part of a fully independent academic and research community. The challenges are considerable, however. The following points may help in considering the development of an effective system of scholarly communication.

1. Scholarly journals cannot be established and gain recognition or durability immediately. They must be provided with adequate funding and support for a period of several years.
2. The local academic community, which has traditionally faced outwards in seeking publication, must be willing to publish at least some material in local journals, which will depend on local scholars for their sustenance. At the same time, academic authorities must encourage local scholars to publish in these journals and provide appropriate rewards for such publication. A sense of intellectual nationalism is necessary, tempered of course by willingness to look outward as well as inward for ideas.
3. Journals must be given a substantial degree of freedom and independence in every respect. In some nations, the tradition of academic freedom may be weak, but a journal will never reach true excellence if it is not permitted considerable autonomy, free of direct political or ideological interference. Such freedom may be tempered by loyalty to the polity and a sensitivity to potentially explosive issues. Even so, those with authority over the journal must make a basic commitment to its intellectual independence. If an editor has to worry constantly about offending political authorities, neither scholarly excellence nor a place among journals of international repute can be achieved.

4. From the beginning, a journal must set a high standard and establish norms and means of operation. If it compromises, it will not build for itself a reputation of excellence, and the best local scholars will prefer to publish elsewhere. The editor must have a sense of values and instill among others the concepts of external review and of acceptance of manuscripts solely on the basis of merit. Such values are easy to discuss in the abstract but sometimes quite difficult to implement in reality. Again, firm commitments and patience are required.

5. Any journal must have a sense of its own purpose and mission. All too often, journals are established without reference to a basic raison d'être and therefore have no clear focus. This is important even when the nature of the academic system and the level of scholarly development might call for an orientation somewhat broader than might be necessary in the West.

6. The language of publication is one of the most important questions facing Third World journals, and one with both financial and editorial implications. If the journal is published in an international language, there is a potential for circulation to and contributions from other countries. But there may be compelling reasons for deciding otherwise, as in Malaysia and Indonesia, where the governments have worked to make the indigenous language the medium of instruction in higher education as well as of national life generally. In such instances, the journals will be restricted in circulation largely to their own countries, limiting their influence and perhaps making local scholars less willing to publish in them. There may also be problems of vocabulary and usage, and in this regard journals can assist in the codification of Third World languages. On the other hand, an international language can attract foreign subscriptions paid for in hard currency; and in a small country, international exposure may mean the difference between a journal's economic survival and collapse.

7. Regional cooperation has been a challenge in the Third World. An experiment in academic and publishing cooperation in East Africa, for example, has not been successful. National feelings run high and political issues may intrude, not to speak of problems of language and logistics. Nonetheless, regional collaborations can be a substantial help to scholarly journals by expanding the base of potential authors as well as subscribers. The *West African Journal of Education* is published in Nigeria but serves a larger market and carries articles relating to other countries in its region. The *Caribbean Journal of Education*, another successful example of regional collaboration, is sponsored by a university that is itself a successful re-

gional institution. In this regard, it might be useful to look at several of the regional journals in Europe, such as the *Scandinavian Journal of Sociology*, for guidelines.

8. Related to the concept of regional publications is the sponsorship of scholarly journals by international and regional organizations. UNESCO and its affiliated bodies may serve as useful examples, although it must be recognized that UNESCO journals such as the *International Journal of Social Science and Prospects* appear in several languages and are accordingly expensive to produce, and furthermore have full-time editorial staffs. Regional organizations in the Third World also publish journals. The Regional Institute of Higher Education and Development (RIHED), in Southeast Asia, for example, maintained a successful publication program for a decade. Regional organizations have a built-in constituency, a large geographical base, and frequently the financial ability to establish a journal. Their sponsorship can provide significant prestige to a new journal and attract authors.
9. Scholarly journals in the Third World may have special difficulties in attracting enough manuscripts of high quality. There are many reasons. Third World academic communities are not as oriented to research and publication as their counterparts in the industrialized nations. There are also fewer scholars. Funds for research are usually very limited. And, as noted, those scholars who do publish often prefer to contribute to the major international journals. Yet local journals must build a base of authorship of sufficient quality to attract other good manuscripts. This is one of the most pressing editorial problems, since without an adequate flow of manuscripts it is impossible to develop a journal that will be taken seriously by the research community within the country and perhaps overseas as well.

10. There is a tendency in many Third World nations for individual academic institutions to establish scholarly journals, which almost inevitably become limited in authorship and circulation to the sponsoring institution and its mailing lists. They are seldom able to develop a wider constituency or establish a national or international reputation. It may be a mistake to provide funds and expend energy on such university-affiliated journals. Limited resources might be better invested in developing journals in specific fields or disciplines on a national or regional basis. This involves careful decisions. The number of journals must necessarily be limited: the research community cannot support too many publications. The field of study of

> any new journal must have an adequate base of scholarship in the country or region and be of interest and relevance to the area. Initiative must, naturally, be mainly in the hands of the scholars themselves, but a broader perspective to reflect national priorities and resources may also be involved.

There are many examples of successful journals published in the Third World to serve as models. *The Journal of Southeast Asian Studies,* for example, has achieved a considerable measure of success by concentrating on topics of direct relevance to its region, focusing on areas in which other journals did not concentrate, attracting authors as well as subscribers on an international basis, and ensuring a high standard of articles. It is considered among the standard journals in its field and has the respect of scholars everywhere. It publishes material which is directly relevant to the region and offers an outlet for publication by scholars from Southeast Asia as well as other parts of the world. It is published in English. In India, several journals devoted to communicating scientific knowledge have been published in various Indian languages with the help of government agencies. They have attracted a substantial and highly educated audience and are able to obtain articles from well-known writers. The *West African Journal of Education,* mentioned earlier, has also become one of the standard publications in its field and, despite its inability to publish on a regular basis, has attracted authors from both Africa and the industrialized West.

Chapter 9

Book Publishing in a Developing Regional Culture: The Case of Maharashtra, India

Books and other printed materials play an important role in the Third World. They contribute to the growth and dissemination of knowledge, they are often integral to the creation of an indigneous political culture, and they are a key to the growth and maintenance of literacy. Central to the issue of providing printed materials is the publishing process.[1] Most of the rather limited attention paid to publishing in the Third World has been focused on books in European languages, since these languages remain the primary publishing languages of most Third World nations. This chapter considers the rather special problems of publishing in an indigenous Third World language, since in the long run book publishing must expand in these languages. Metropolitan languages currently serve only a small elite, and the large majority of the population is cut off from knowledge communicated through these languages. In India, for example, it is estimated that about 2 percent of the population is literate in English—the language in which approximately half of the books are published and the language of the major newspapers and magazines. The overall literacy rate is 40 percent, low by the standards of industrialized nations but significantly higher than for English. Literacy in indigenous languages, however, is divided among more than fifteen major languages.

This chapter seeks to examine publishing, and by implication knowledge distribution, in one of India's major regional languages, Marathi, the mother tongue of 50 million people. The problems faced by publishers in these developing regional cultures are very different from those experienced by the metropolitan languages—and very little is known about them.[2] As literacy rates slowly rise, they increase mainly in indigenous languages, thereby creating a need for printed materials—and a market for them as well.[3]

In addition, the history of colonialism weighs heavily on many Third World nations.[4] Publishing enterprises were in general established by Europeans, and thus their orientations are often Western in nature. Regional languages, which are keys to building an indigenous publishing industry, often receive a low priority. The language issue is central to understanding Marathi publishing. Subjects traditionally presented in the English medium—science and current events—continue to have considerable impact on the market, thereby limiting the scope for the expansion of Marathi publishing.

A WORD ON INDIAN PUBLISHING

Established under British colonialism and dominated for many years by foreign firms and foreign norms, the controlling element of Indian publishing remains the English-language houses, although these firms have all been "Indianized."[5] The large publishers located in Delhi, Bombay, and, to a lesser extent, Calcutta and Madras dominated publishing in terms of established norms and orientations. Publishing in India is by now well established, and India is the eighth-largest publishing nation in the world, and by far the largest publisher in the Third World. Indian books are used in other Third World nations, and the necessary infrastructures of printing facilities, paper suppliers, editorial expertise, and to some extent distribution arrangements (although distribution remains the weak link in Indian publishing) exist in the English-language sector of Indian publishing.

Publishing in India's fifteen regional languages is newer and less well established. Virtually all of the discussion of Indian publishing has thus far been concerned with English-language publishing, and thus relatively little is known about regional-language publishing. Regional-language publishing is growing and is very slowly coming to be an important element in the country's cultural structure. The proportion of books published in English has been modestly declining in recent years. For example, the total Indian reading public in 1973 was approximately 77.5 million in all languages, with about 12 million literate in English. Of a total of 17,020 book titles published in 1972–73, 7,314 were issued in English. Thus, 43 percent of the book titles were published for 16 percent of the reading public (and 2 percent of the total population). Marathi, which is the third-largest publishing language in India, had 1,231 titles issued in 1972–73. This constituted about 7 percent of the total titles published according to certain statistics (conflicting figures also exist). Hindi, the second largest publishing language and mother tongue of just under half of the Indian population (but only about one-quarter of the literate population) accounted for 2,825 (17 percent) of the book titles published. The inequality in publishing is evident from these statistics. Even the most developed publishing languages, such as Bengali, Malayalam, and Marathi, suffer significant disadvantages when compared to English.

Not only are the regional languages at a numerical disadvantage, but the kinds of books published are limited in scope. Almost all books on advanced scientific subjects, whether in the natural or social sciences, are published in English. Most postgraduate textbooks and supplementary volumes are published in English. A large proportion of the books on current events are issued in English. The regional languages and Hindi have a disproportionate offering of books on religion, literature, cultural affairs, and popular novels and self-help books. Most school textbooks are now published in the regional languages, as are an increasing number of college texts. But the books required for postgraduate study and for research work are still almost exclusively in English, even in fields such as sociology, which are in the process of shifting the medium of instruction to the regional language at the postgraduate level in many universities.

THE MAHARASHTRA CONTEXT

The state of Maharashtra provides a cultural and economic context which determines the status of its publishing industry. With a population of 50 million, Maharashtra is one of India's larger states. The official state language, Marathi, is the mother tongue of a large majority of the population. Marathi, which is Sanskrit based and written in the Devanagari script, has a long literary and intellectual tradition. Maharashtra was established in 1960, after a long struggle by the

Marathi-speaking community to have a state based on the use of their language. Thus, the very existence of Maharashtra is a tribute to the commitment to Marathi language and culture as well as to other factors. Maharashtrians also have an important political culture, dating back to the leadership of Shivaji, who dominated much of central India in the seventeenth century. Maharashtrians have a reputation for industriousness, thrift, and a commitment to culture, reflected in the high level of literacy (50 percent) and a flourishing educational system. Even on a world scale, Marathi is not an insignificant language. It has, for example, many more speakers than Dutch or Swedish, and is on a par with Italian.

Maharashtra is dominated by two centers: Bombay and Poona. Bombay, the capital of the state, has a population of over 8 million. It is a polyglot city which, although dominated by a Marathi-speaking population, includes large numbers of Gujaratis, Parsis, South Indians, and others whose mother tongue is not Marathi. As it is the key commercial city in India, English is of continuing importance as the major language of commerce. The city's major newspapers are in English and the city's financial elite is mostly non-Maharashtrian. Bombay is also an important publishing center. The University of Bombay, one of the oldest in India and one of the most prestigious, has chosen to keep most of its academic programs in English rather than shifting to Marathi. Without question, Bombay dominates Maharashtra financially, commercially, and industrially. It is the seat of the state government and contains many of the key intellectual institutions, both English and Marathi.

The other center is Poona, the traditional seat of Marathi culture and power and still an intellectual center of importance in the state. Several key Marathi publishers and cultural institutions are located there, and the city, which has a population of about 1 million, has a lively cultural life. Unlike Bombay, Poona's intellectual climate is almost exclusively Maharashtrian, and the Marathi language plays a larger role. The rest of the state, with 75 percent of the population, has a very small intellectual life and has few publishers or centers of culture. Indeed, the lack of bookstores and the limited number of libraries outside of Bombay or Poona cause substantial problems for the growth of the publishing industry.

The orientation of Maharashtrian culture and the configurations of the state's intellectual and cultural life help to determine the nature of its publishing industry. Maharashtra's income level is one of the highest in India, but the city of Bombay accounts for a substantial part of this wealth. While the state has a fairly well-developed library system, with about 1,400 in all, most of the village libraries purchase few books. Perhaps 220 libraries try to keep fairly current in terms of book purchases of Marathi publications. While English-language readership tends to be concentrated in the cities and fairly accessible to the retail bookshops, Marathi readers are much more dispersed and more difficult to reach.

Marathi culture has a strong intellectual tradition, but this has been directed more at the theatre and literary magazines than toward books. The publishing industry has had to attempt to instil a book consciousness in a population which is not used to purchasing books. In this sense, Maharashtra differs from Bengal and Kerala, where books have played a more important traditional role. In addition, those most able to afford books often prefer to purchase reading materials in English. In Maharashtra, many of these persons are not Marathi-speaking in any case. In general, there is more prestige attached to reading English than any Indian language. Thus, Marathi culture is for the most part middle class and thus far has not emphasized books as a means of cultural or intellectual exchange.

THE SCOPE OF MARATHI PUBLISHING

Marathi publishing originated with a Christian missionary, and the first book printed was a Marathi-English dictionary in 1805.[6] These beginnings are rather typical of publishing in many Third World languages. Many of the early Marathi books served the spread of Christianity. Although a Marathi-speaking state did not emerge until 1960, political encouragement for literature in Marathi began in 1956, when a bilingual Bombay state was established. Cultural reformers of the late nineteenth century as well as political and cultural nationalists of the twentieth century stressed, to some extent, the importance of Marathi as a medium of expression. Thus, Marathi journals and newspapers have existed in Bombay, Poona, and several other large towns for a century or more.

Recent developments have provided a firmer base for intellectual enterprise in Marathi, but a significant contradiction exists. On the one hand, official policy has favored the expansion of Marathi cultural and intellectual expression, but on the other the pressure to retain English is very strong. The establishment of a Marathi-speaking state was, of course, a key factor. Other elements which contributed to the growth of Marathi intellectual life—and also of publishing—included the following: central government grants of some 10 million rupees for fostering textbooks in Marathi, the gradual expansion of literacy in Marathi, the shift of most of the schools and many colleges and some universities to a Marathi medium, the continued growth of the Marathi theatre, and the policies of the government of Maharashtra.[7]

There are also powerful pressures against the rapid growth of Marathi as the dominant intellectual language in the state. The desire of intellectuals to reach a wide audience, in India as well as abroad, militates against the use of Marathi. The fact that advanced education at the postgraduate level in most fields, especially the sciences, remains in English also influences authors. The almost complete domination of private-sector business and commerce by English maintains its status as the prestige language.

While there are no firm statistics on the scope of Marathi publishing, it is possible to make some sound estimates. There are about two hundred Marathi publishers, but only fifteen to twenty-five of these are classified as big by most observers. And a big publisher in Marathi issues only ten or more new titles per year. The large majority issue only a few titles annually and are primarily in other business—usually bookselling or distributing. Several English-language publishers issue a few titles in Marathi, but should probably not be classified as full-scale Marathi publishers. There are fewer than five fully professional Marathi publishers, with a full-time editorial staff and a business which is primarily devoted to publishing books in Marathi. Thus, as several observers have pointed out, Marathi publishing is not professional in the established sense of the term. It remains an enterprise attached to other kinds of work. The entire ethos and operation of Marathi publishing is affected by this reality. Virtually no general (trade) publishers depend on book publishing for their primary source of revenue. However, there are a number of full-time publishers who focus on the production of textbooks and self-help publications.

Professionally trained personnel are rare in Marathi publishing. Most publishers are family firms which have only a few employees devoted to publishing, and these often have other responsibilities in addition to publishing. Relatively few Maharashtrian publishers seem to be involved in the professional publishing community in India; this has hindered the growth of an effective publishing infrastructure. A new Poona-based organization, the Marathi Prakashak Parishad (Marathi Publishers' Association), has recently been established and indicates a growing professional consciousness.

Most publishing firms tend to be very small, with an output of just a few titles annually. There is relatively little effort to distribute these books, and the printings are small. On the other hand, overheads are low and the publication of a single title is a relatively limited financial risk for most publishers. It is estimated that an average printing for a Marathi book, except for textbooks, is around 1,000 copies. Books often remain in print for a decade or more, and sell quite slowly. But since the numbers of books involved is limited, there are few efforts at careful cost accounting. The publishing operation is done on an avocational basis and there is less economic pressure to produce quick profits—or in many cases, any profits at all.

The markets for books in Marathi are limited and rather specialized, and the perceptions of these markets play a major role in determining what is published and in deciding on the size of editions. As with all books in India, libraries purchase most Marathi books. There are probably 200 public and state-supported libraries in the state which attempt to maintain a high level of book acquisition in Marathi. Most village libraries, which number around 1,000, probably account for relatively few book purchases. In addition, there are more than 700 colleges in Maharashtra, and some college libraries purchase a limited number of Marathi-language books. Such purchases are probably higher in rural and town colleges, which have expanded rapidly in recent years, since Marathi tends often to be the instructional medium in such colleges. But college library purchasing is normally limited and specialized to some extent.

It is widely assumed that scientific and technical books will have no market in Marathi, and that books in the social sciences will sell poorly. Publishers believe that most institutional as well as private purchasers prefer books in English on these topics. Sales statistics apparently support these perceptions, and as a result private publishers are seldom willing to publish any scholarly or technical books in Marathi. Publishers perceive the market for Marathi books to be in the areas of fiction, cultural commentary and criticism, religion, and to some extent in popular books on current political and social affairs. Curiously, books on poetry sell fairly well in Marathi. Titles selling over 3,000 copies in a year or so are considered best-sellers. Magazines have a substantial circulation in Maharashtra, although they are by no means as popular as in Tamilnad or Bengal. A number of publishers issue magazines and journals as well as books. Marathi writers have developed the essay to a high level, and magazines are good outlets for literary or political essays. Many of these magazines are published on an annual basis at the time of major holidays and are, in a sense, book-length collections of essays on a range of topics. The magazine format also has the advantage of including advertisements, which help to defray the costs of publication. It has been estimated that there are as many as 500 different magazines of this type, with circulations ranging from fewer than 1,000 to 6,000 or more. A few are regularly published, such as *Kirloskars,* which sells about 20,000 copies per monthly issue, but most are less frequently issued and have smaller circulations. A recent decision by the business house that owns *Kirloskars* to close it down, along with several other Marathi publications, will have a negative effect on the fragile journal network in the language. In a sense, authors are used to writing for journals, and readers are accustomed to buying them. It has been somewhat difficult for books to break into a market dominated by the magazines and other cultural forms.

Distribution is probably the weakest link in the chain of Indian publishing generally, and it is an especially serious difficulty for the regional languages.[8] The number of book titles are limited and the topics on which Marathi books are published restricted; thus, booksellers have a difficult time making sufficient profits from Marathi books. The network of relatively efficient wholesalers which provide national distribution for books in English is by and large lacking for Marathi publications. In general, the distribution network functions best for books which provide the highest profits (imported books), and worst for volumes which are least profitable, the regional language publications.[9]

It has been estimated that there are approximately fifteen bookshops in Bombay and another twenty-five in Poona which carry a fairly wide selection of Marathi books. Beyond these few shops, it is extraordinarily difficult to obtain Marathi books without ordering them from the publisher. The smaller bookshops outside the major metropolitan centres generate most of their income from textbooks and from non-book items. Such bookshops as attempt seriously to provide some diversity of stock are geared mainly to serving the library market. Since this market has been eroded by wholesalers who have attempted, with some success, to sell directly to libraries by offering better discounts, the retail bookshops have been placed under tremendous economic pressure. Booksellers, in part because their economic mainstay is not in selling trade books, take little initiative. Their selection is very limited indeed, and they are reluctant to special-order books for individual customers, in part because postal rates for books are very high.

The distribution network produces a self-perpetuating cycle of poverty in the book trade. The failure of publishers to offer profitable discounts, to court the booksellers, and to provide them with information about their books means that the incentive to remain abreast of current books and to stock a good selection is very limited.

The economics of Marathi publishing is difficult to fully discern, but a few generalizations can be made. The investment per title is relatively small in most cases. It is estimated that an average of $1,000 to $4,000 must be invested in a normal 250-page volume in a printing of between 1,000 and 2,000.[10] Printing costs for Marathi are somewhat lower than for English, primarily since much Marathi printing is done in Poona, where costs in general are lower than in Bombay. Marathi publishers almost invariably use poorer-quality paper than is common for books in English, and hand-binding is universal. Since publishers employ few professionals and do little advertising or publicity, overheads are significantly lower than in English-language publishing in India. All of these economies permit lower production costs.

In addition, the discount structure for Marathi books is different than for English books, and this structure permits lower retail costs. The costing ratio for Marathi books tends to be 1 : 3, or setting the retail price at three times the actual cost of the volume. In English-language publishing, the ratio tends to be 1 : 4 or 1 : 5. There are lower discounts to booksellers and wholesalers—and thus lower profits for book distributors. This is but one reason for the relatively under-developed distribution network for Marathi books. Booksellers will naturally prefer to handle English-language books, since they make more money in selling them. Books in English command a discount of 40 percent or more, while Marathi books are generally handled at a 30 percent discount. The economic equation is, of course, complicated.

The economics of authorship in Marathi is also a problem for publishers. While the royalty rates tend to be similar to those in English, 10 to 15 percent being standard, lower unit prices for books and small editions mean that authors do not earn much money. In addition, Marathi books take a very long time to sell, and thus payment is spread. Most authors who write in Marathi are also capable of writing in English, and some prefer English simply because it is more remunerative. In many cases, authors who are not well established command even lower royalties or their work is purchased on a flat-fee basis by publishers. There is the perennial problem in Indian publishing of late payment of even these modest royalties. It is probably fair to observe that authorship, like publishing itself, is something of an avocation, a labor of love rather than a serious professional undertaking. The situation for a few authors has recently improved to some degree. The establishment of several literary prizes, the sale of translation rights, and in a few cases fees paid by recording firms and copyright earnings from performances have all added to the incomes of a small number of well-known Marathi authors.

Several innovative Marathi publishers have attempted to use alternative means of selling their books, but with limited success. Several book clubs have been started in recent years as a means of circumventing the distribution apparatus, lowering prices to readers, or providing the publishers with a means of guaranteeing sales. The oldest book club in Marathi is sponsored by Popular Prakashan, one of the largest Marathi publishers which also has a large English-language publishing enterprise, a printing press, and several bookshops. The Bombay Book Club offers about 600 titles to its 2,000 members.

A more recent development is the Readers' Movement (Granthali), which was founded by several Marathi authors. Their aim is to publish a limited number of titles per year for members. While it is too early to judge the success of this effort, about five books have been published in editions of about 2,000 copies and offered to members at about 5 rupees per copy and to the general public at 10 to 15 rupees. The Granthali, as a volunteer effort of committed authors, has little overhead, so it is difficult to judge the book club by the usual economic criteria. It does indicate, however, that there is a consciousness about the prices of books and the means of distribution among at least a few writers and journalists. An early effort at efficient book distribution was the Marathi Grantha Prakashak Sabha, a publishers' cooperative which attempted, without dramatic success, to improve book distribution channels. In addition, several publishers, at present most notably Continental Prakashan of Poona, use their own vans to distribute and sell books in rural areas.

GOVERNMENT INVOLVEMENT

Government initiative and participation is an important element in Third World publishing, and the situation in Maharashtra is no exception. For example, the decision several years ago to nationalize textbook publishing at the school level had widespread and deep implications for private-sector publishing. One of the major and most remunerative markets for books was immediately removed. The school text market was especially important in that it could guarantee a fairly quick return on investment and distribution networks were well established. Government policy was aimed at reducing the costs of books and at ensuring greater control over both the production and writing of texts. But one of the implications was severly to cripple private-sector publishing. Without the relatively lucrative text market, private publishers could not bring out significant numbers of general books.

Several government agencies are concerned with book publishing and distribution. The Maharashtra State Board for Literature and Culture has a broad responsibility for the "general stimulation of Marathi culture and literature." The University Textbook Committee has a more limited responsibility for the production and distibution of textbooks, mainly at the post-secondary level. A grant of 10 million rupees to the Textbook Committee was made by the central government and this permitted the substantial development of textbooks. Maharashtra was able to use its grant (a similar amount was provided to each state) fairly effectively.

The coordinating agency for book development is the Maharashtra State Board for Literature and Culture, with its headquarters in Bombay. Founded in 1960, the board has wide responsibilities, including the general stimulation of Marathi culture and literature, book publication in fields of culture, language, sciences, and the arts, and preparation of key reference books in Marathi.[11] The major project of the board has been the sponsorship of a twenty-volume Marathi encyclopedia, patterned after the *Encyclopaedia Britannica*. Eight of the projected twenty volumes have so far been published. In addition, the board has sponsored several other reference projects, with the aim of providing Marathi readers with access to a world knowledge base. The board has sponsored the translation of major world classics into Marathi. Many of these volumes are published by private publishers with subsidies from the board. The board pays for the translations and subsidizes the printing costs so that the selling prices are modest. The board also sponsors the preparation of books in the applied sciences and in practical areas. Volumes on radio repair, elementary physics, and similar topics are published under board auspices.

The board assists private publishers through its subsidy programs. Its annual budget of approximately 2.5 million rupees has permitted the publication of about a dozen new titles each year. Other books are partially aided by board funds. Most of the editions are fairly small, similar to commercial presses, but occasionally books are published in larger numbers. The board also assists authors by providing opportunities for translation and for subsidized writing. The encyclopedia project has involved a large number of Maharashtrian intellectuals. The overall impact of the board on Marathi publishing is not very large, but it has assisted in the publication of over 100 volumes which probably would otherwise not have been published.

Another government body, the Maharashtra University Textbook Production Board, which has been funded through the University Grants Commission for the most part, has undertaken the publication of college and university-level textbooks and supplementary materials in the sciences and social sciences. Most of the books are originals, but some are translations from English. These volumes are published by private firms with financing from the university board, and are distributed through normal commercial channels. In the past seven years, this program has published more than 160 volumes. Authors benefit since they are paid standard book royalties of 15 percent.[12]

While it is difficult to evaluate the overall role of government in Marathi publishing, it is possible that the single act of nationalizing school-level textbooks was a blow so damaging to private publishers that all of the other assistance provided has not made up for it. None of the government initiatives have been directly aimed at helping the private publishing sector.

Marathi publishing has, over fifty years, succeeded in establishing itself as an integral part of the Maharashtrian intellectual scene. Basic infrastructures exist; there are printing facilities, a minimal distribution network, and a number of publishers (and others) willing to take the risk of issuing books. The potential for further development is, without question, quite strong. As levels of literacy rise and as the middle class grows and expands from the larger towns and cities to smaller towns in the state, and as the centers of intellectual life gradually shift from English to Marathi (and the other regional languages), there will be a larger market for books. And there will be a much more urgent need for them. The current shift of the medium of instruction in the schools to Marathi, especially outside the urban areas, is especially significant.

Despite these long-term prospects, most observers of the book trade are not very optimistic about the immediate future. The performance of the publishing industry to date has been mixed. Although it has established itself against considerable odds, there is a lack of professionalism and a very serious problem of book distribution. A few publishers possess reasonable expertise, and a few have played an active—and sometimes a leading—role in Marathi intellectual life, but most cannot be considered to have an important function in these areas. The role of government has been ambiguous, and the intellectual community itself looks in different directions at once. There is little book consciousness, and not much has been done to develop it.

Marathi, like other Third World languages, finds itself in a triply peripheral position. Not only is Marathi a small language on the world scale, but it also functions in a society of scarcity, where the technologies of printing, book distribution, and the like are not as yet very well developed. Book technology, in relation to the purchasing power of the public, is expensive. Further, literacy rates are fairly low and much of the population is excluded from printed material for this reason. Finally, Marathi functions in a national and international market dominated by English. In India, English-speaking publishers and multinational firms dominate the scene. The large Delhi and Bombay firms have the most professional operations; they set standards for regional languages publishing, often to the detriment of the indigenous languages. They have a major role in book imports and exports, a critical element of the book trade. They dominate such elements as copyright policy, wholesaling, and distribution networks. They are able to siphon off the best talent, in terms of publishing expertise and also authors, and they are better able to obtain commercial financing.

Thus, Marathi publishing functions within concentric circles of disadvantage. It is not part of the international publishing network dominated by the industrialized nations using world languages such as English, French, and to some extent German and Spanish. These nations control the international book trade, have dominated copyright arrangements, and have determined book pricing and distribution practices. Marathi publishers are also at a disadvantage in the context of Indian publishing, which is controlled to a considerable degree by English and to some extent Hindi firms. And Marathi publishing functions in the context of a poor and only partly literate regional culture. That publishing in Marathi has developed as effectively as it has is itself impressive. The basis for a viable publishing industry now exists and is contributing actively to Maharashtrian intellectual and educational life. The period up to the mid-1970s can be seen as that of the development of an infrastructure. While it is not clear that a take-off point has been reached, the industry now has the basic facilities it needs.

It may be appropriate to conclude this chapter by raising a basic question concerning the publishing industry in the Third World. This analysis, written by a sympathetic observer of the Indian scene, is based on implicit assumptions concerning the nature of publishing, books, and the distribution of knowledge. These assumptions are Western in nature, and reflect the historical development of publishing and knowledge distribution in Europe and North America. They are also the assumptions on which the Indian publishing industry is based and which virtually all Indian publishers share today.

Among these assumptions are ideas about the nature of a book in terms of paper quality, printing excellence, and design. We assume that books must be professionally edited and distributed through networks familiar in Western terms. We assume that books, in general, must pay their own way in terms of earning a profit or at least not losing money for those producing them. We assume that the book is the logical means of communication rather than magazines, pamphlets, etc. And we assume that print media are the basic forms of communication.

Many of these assumptions are justified, but it may be useful to step back from established practice and think about other models. Some alternative examples do exist: in the Indian context, a highly successful cooperative publishing house owned by Malayalam authors in Kerala, the Sahitya Pravartaka Shakarana Sangam, is based on somewhat different assumptions. In Nigeria, the emergence of self-publishing ventures aimed at a popular audience represent another publishing alternative. Soviet book policy is also based on assumptions somewhat different from general Western concepts, in that less stress is placed on economic returns and more on political and social uses of knowledge.[13] And even in the United States, a new trend towards 'alternative' publishing and self-publishing exists side by side with the takeover of publishing companies by large multipurpose corporations.[14]

Chapter 10

Access to Knowledge Networks: Problems and Possibilities for Southeast Asian Scholarly Books

Publishers in the Third World are inherently at a disadvantage in an international context dominated by the industrialized nations of the West.[1] Yet the scholarship of the Third World must reach the First. Reaching that goal will require cooperation between academic communities on both sides. This chapter recognizes the basically unequal system for distribution of knowledge in the world. Yet it holds out considerable optimism that, through cooperation, much can be done to ensure that books from Southeast Asia, and other developing nations, can be distributed more successfully internationally.

Scholarly books published in the Third World frequently reflect viewpoints different from those of the West or deal with questions directly relevant to emerging economies. They provide a necessary outlet for Third World scholars, who may have problems dealing with publishers in the industrialized West. Often a study that is not published regionally will not be published at all, for lack of interest elsewhere. Yet books from the Third World require an international market, for the local or even regional market may be too small to support the costs of publishing a specialized monograph.[2]

The basic fact about the international system of knowledge is its inequality. The control over international scholarly communication is firmly in the hands of the Western industrialized nations. There are many reasons for this situation, among them the location of the major publishing houses, journals, data bases, and other resources. The libraries and expertise of such institutions as the School of Oriental and African Studies, the John M. Echols collection at Cornell, and programs on the South Asian societies at Chicago and UCLA are in the West. So are the headquarters of multinational publishing houses—Oxford University Press, Longmans, McGraw-Hill, Prentice-Hall, and Harper & Row, to mention only a few—which continue to play an important role in Southeast Asia.[3]

The major Western publishers cater in general to their largest and most immediate markets—the Western scholarly communities, where most of their authors are also to be found.[4] The major scholarly journals are edited in the industrialized nations, and their editors, reviewers, and most of their readers as well are located there.[5] The concerns of these publishers are determined by their location, by locally dominant research paradigms, and by their readers, writers, and editors. All these factors make it difficult for a Third World scholar to gain access to the major international journals and book publishers.

This structural inequality is compounded in the market. The bulk of the world's research materials is purchased by institutional buyers, mainly libraries, in the industrialized nations. This market buys in a limited number of languages—mainly English and French, plus some German, Spanish, and Russian. There is major resistance to buying books in other languages. The libraries, moreover, primarily buy books from the major publishing nations and resist books from other nations. They buy journals which are internationally recognized and which are recommended by faculty members. It is accordingly difficult for Southeast Asian books and journals, as well as authors, to gain access to the West.

The major metropolitan languages, English and French, tend to dominate international scholarly communication, with Spanish playing a much less important role, largely in Latin America, and Russian being influential in its area of political domination and certain disciplinary areas. The bulk of the internationally circulated scholarly books and journals is published in English. Scholars who wish to reach an international audience tend increasingly to write in these languages. Increasingly, publishers in nonmetropolitan areas are issuing materials in English or French. In the Third World, local journals are frequently published in a metropolitan language, and universities often demand that scholars publish in an international journal to be eligible for promotion. The major international data bases are also in the metropolitan languages, and many abstracting and reference services, such as the ERIC system in the United States, tend to cover material only in the major Western languages, mainly English. Scholarly publishers in Southeast Asia who seek access to an international audience must publish in English, and even then can rarely expect more than a small, specialized institutional sale. Books published in regional languages will be of interest only to specialized research-based institutions.

The norms and values of much scholarship, and consequently of publication, also tend to be Western. Quantitative social science, for example, dominates American sociology and political science and the major U.S. journals in those fields. Third World scholars who do not have access to computer facilities to analyse data, or find it difficult to collect that kind of data, or feel that local realities make other approaches to research more appropriate, may have great difficulty getting published in international forums.

The Third World has only limited funds for scholarly books and journals, and a disproportionate amount of that is taken up by purchases of publications from the West. Local publishers frequently depend on foreign sales when deciding to publish a book: for instance, Indian scholarly publishers assume that a significant portion of their modest press runs, sometimes up to one-half, will be sold overseas, largely in North America and Britain. This means that the books published in the Third World are determined, at least in part, by the local perception of interest in a foreign marketplace. Only a few networks permit scholarly books published in one part of the Third World to be circulated effectively in another. Generally, the pattern of trade still follows the old colonial ties—from North to South rather than South to South.

Western governments and the major information corporations see their interests in the maintenance of the status quo and try, in general, to augment their domination of the communication networks. Foreign-assistance programs in education, for example, have frequently included the exports of books and scientific material of all kinds. The multinational publishers have to some extent decentralized their operations in the Third World and have done some impressive local publishing, but much of their turnover remains the export of books of all kinds from the metropole to the Third World.[6]

Third World publishers have cause to fear U.S. initiatives. Following

Curtis Benjamin's 1984 report, *U.S. Books Abroad: Neglected Ambassadors,* the United States Information Agency has emphasized the important ideological role of books and has argued that the United States has "unilaterally disarmed in the use of American books overseas." A task force has recommended that the U.S. government appropriate $20 million a year to finance the movement of American books into difficult markets in target countries by subsidizing selected institutional buyers and by using currency-convertible guarantees. It further recommended that subscriptions to academic and scholarly journals be provided to leading academics and professionals overseas to give them a sense of collegiality with their American counterparts and to provide them with information about current books and research in their fields. Foreign governments would be encouraged to make available matching dollar exchange to import U.S. books.[7]

Important intellectual and commercial consequences will flow from moves to implement these policies. The impact of the British ELBS (English Language Book Scheme) and Russian English-language publishing schemes is well known. It is not as if no foundation-aided flow is in place. The Asia Foundation alone made available in 1982 to developing countries $8 million worth of books under its Books for Asia program.[8] At a time when Third World publishers and academics are awakening to their responsibilities, the U.S. move will undercut their efforts. The Third World academic will become a renewed target in an ideological war (*The Bookseller* argues for a suitable British response). The need more than ever is for Western academics to support what is being attempted in scholarly publishing in the Third World. Who will speak up for true collegiality?

Compared with other Third World regions, Southeast Asia has some important advantages in the development of scholarly publishing and the potential to distribute its knowledge internationally through books and journals. The region's academic community has grown and matured impressively over the last two decades.[9] In every Southeast Asian country governments have invested heavily in higher education. Not only has the number of conventional academic institutions increased, but the acceptance of the open university concept, for example, in Indonesia and Thailand has led to a dramatic growth in student numbers.

The expansion has necessarily led to recruitment of new faculty members, and thus to an increase in the community available to undertake research. Not all countries have been able to rely on their own citizens, and Singapore, for instance, has recruited staff extensively from abroad. More importantly, there has been considerable diversification in the types of courses offered at the tertiary level: new areas of teaching and research include accounting, estate management, rural sociology, and business administration. One publisher recently estimated that some thirty-five hundred courses were taught in Malaysian universities and that between two and three thousand tertiary-level textbooks were required to teach courses satisfactorily in the indigenous language. Specialized research centers are also expanding. Malaysia, for instance, has over the years built up an impressive capacity for research in tropical crops, and the Rubber Research Institute is justifiably world famous. The Philippines plays host to the International Rice Research Institute. Singapore's Institute of Southeast Asian Studies is emerging as a major center for research into Southeast Asia and has an ambitious publishing program. Both Malaysia and Indonesia have important centers for strategic studies. Such specialized research centers are major sources of new knowledge in addition to the universities, though not all have publishing facilities.

As part of this growth, Southeast Asian academe has grown increasingly international. More than a hundred thousand Southeast Asian students study abroad, and large numbers of academics pursue higher degrees abroad. Not only Westerners are contributing to improved understanding of national and regional issues: numerous Indian academics have an interest in Southeast Asia, and Thailand, for instance, plays host to a large number of Japanese academics. Internationalism is further aided by the active interest of UNESCO and such agencies as the Asia and Ford Foundations, the International Development Research Centre, the Toyota Foundation, and the Volkswagen Foundation, and regional groupings such as the Southeast Asian Ministers of Education Organization (SEAMEO), the Association of Southeast Asian Institutions of Higher Learning (ASAIHL), and the Regional Institute of Higher Education and Development (RIHED).

As one result of this internationalization, many First World research interests, paradigms, orientations, and texts are commonplace in the Southeast Asian academic community. There has been a reaction to this widespread adoption of Western knowledge. Southeast Asian social scientists are increasingly sceptical of the value assumptions of much Western social science theory, which they claim have been proved inadequate in the light of sociopolitical realities in many developing countries. The enlarged research community is adding much valuable data on developing societies, and the once-supreme Western knowledge sets are being rapidly indigenized.[10] Increasing attention is also being given to the recovery, where applicable, of indigenous scholarly traditions and concerns: in Malaysia, for instance, a call has been made for more attention to Islamic knowledge and indeed to 'revealed knowledge.'

The knowledge that is being generated in Third World academic centers is of more than regional consequence. It affects the way the rest of the world understands historical and contemporary sociopolitical phenomena in developing societies. Examples are the early development of dependency theory in Latin America and the important theoretical and empirical contributions made by Indian economists in classical and development economics. Southeast Asia has produced its own group of outstanding scholars—Constantino and Ileto in the Philippines, Thaemsuk Nammanon and Chattip Nartsupha in Thailand, Husain Ali in Malaysia, and Onghokham and Pramoed Ananta Toer in Indonesia, among others—who are helping to develop new perspectives, especially in Southeast Asian studies. And it is scholarly publishing in these countries that will make this knowledge available to the global community, for metropolitan publishing houses show little interest in Third World scholarship.

A major problem for Southeast Asian academics and publishers is the issue of language. The colonial intrusion has left behind a legacy of metropolitan languages—English, French, Dutch, and Spanish. Some familiarity with these languages may be important for research in the various countries, and much of the research for global consumption must be transmitted in English. But this poses a dilemma. Universities often insist that academics prove their worth by getting articles and manuscripts accepted by internationally known publishers; yet the same scholar may also be under pressure to publish in his or her own national language. Except for the Philippines and Singapore, the expansion of higher education has been an expansion in the indigenous language. There is a vast and as yet unfilled need for course materials and texts in those languages, and it is in this area that most attention in the region's academic publishing is focused. Thailand in particular has had a long tradition of publishing and translating texts for use in tertiary education; Malaysia's Dewan Bahasa dan Pustaka and other commercial publishers have demonstrated that it is possible to shift to an indigenous language of instruction without an excessive drop in standards for lack of texts. Malaysia has by no means solved its shortage of texts, but the systematic way in which the problems have been tackled promises much.[11] Indigenous-language publishing is bound to be helped by the growing number of readers who have been educated in their own language education system and who are, moreover, becoming more actively involved in national affairs. In Indonesia, for instance, the public institutions of higher learning graduate more than twenty-five thousand students annually, almost a quarter of them in the social sciences. However, there will be serious consequences to the international dissemination of knowledge if scholarly publishers in the ASEAN region turn away from English-language publishing.

The scholarly publishing scene in Southeast Asia presents a mixed picture.[12] In Singapore the University of Singapore Press and the Institute of Southeast Asian Studies are major publishers whose books meet international production standards; the extensive use of English means that access to international and regional markets is enhanced. The Philippines has a long tradition of research-based publishing and three major university presses; higher education is largely in English, but increasing attention is being given to the writing of tertiary-level texts and research monographs in Pilipino. Malaysian university presses have adapted to the shift to Bahasa Malaysia; Malaysian tertiary institutions had by 1985 published about 175 titles, while the Dewan Bahasa was responsible for some 330 titles, most of them texts, literary works, or translations.

Thailand and Indonesia have less advanced tertiary publishing sectors. The great majority of titles in Thailand are published in Thai, and there is a fairly substantial number of translations. University press publishing is of recent origin; in addition, several commercial publishers publish academic texts. Indonesia, which seems the most disadvantaged, has at least six university presses and several private-sector academic publishers, but the university presses are not yet as productive as the commercial publishers. Figures culled from UNESCO annual book production statistics indicate that in 1982 about one hundred university theses were published, and that in 1983 about fifty-six were published.[13]

Some significant progress has been made in scholarly journals. Journal publication is in some ways less demanding than a book-publishing program and has the advantage of faster production, relatively lower cost, and a special value to newer disciplines or interdisciplinary areas. Both Singapore and the Philippines have their share of major journals. Singapore publishes the *Journal of Southeast Asian Studies* and the *Singapore Journal of Tropical Geography*—both have an international reputation.[14] The *Philippine Journal of Linguistics,* the *Philippine Social Science and Humanities Review, Philippine Studies, Solidarity,* and the *Journal of History* are major Philippine journals. Among Malaysian journals of significance are the *Journal of the Malaysian Branch of the Royal Asiatic Society, Tenggara, Nusantara,* and the *Rubber Research Institute of Malaysia Journal.* Indonesia has *Annals Bogorienses* and *Menara Perkebunan* (both associated with the Bogor Botanical Garden, an internationally renowed research institution), *Reinwardita,* and *Majalah Kedoktoran Indonesia* (the Indonesian Medical Journal), founded in 1852.

If the achievements are noteworthy, many problems remain. Textbooks are especially needed in the indigenous languages, and in many countries translation is being abandoned in favor of original writing. Even though there are more students, many cannot afford to buy textbooks. For scholarly books the market is even smaller, and the export market is hard to crack; sales of only two to three hundred copies can make a difference, but even getting them reviewed is difficult. Finally, it must be remembered that Southeast Asian publishing is still underdeveloped. There is a lack of editorial, management, and production skills and a shortage of well-written manuscripts.

There are several steps that Southeast Asian publishers could take to improve the dissemination of knowledge from the periphery to the core, and particularly to the United States. The following suggestions are not intended as a blueprint; but perhaps they may stimulate further analysis and constructive action by scholarly publishers, North and South.

1. Seek actively to copublish with U.S. publishers. Several university presses and commercial publishers have demonstrated an interest in Southeast Asian materials, and a shared imprint would increase sales.
2. Pool resources at the national level both for production and for distribution and sales abroad. A larger and wider range of books would be more appealing to a U.S. distributor, and the academic publishing output from a country would make a greater impact.

3. Prepare a catalogue of selected academic/scholarly titles in English from publishers in the ASEAN region, and appoint an international distributor to handle them.

4. Exhibit jointly at international trade fairs like the Frankfurt Book Fair and at annual meetings of the Asian Studies Association, the American Booksellers Association, the American Library Association, and similar organizations.

5. Work more closely with national and regional library associations to keep librarians informed regularly of new publications. Publishers also need to identify and serve more efficiently the specialist bookshops and purchasing agents.

6. Encourage the agencies funding research and conferences to pay more attention to publication. Instead of a single volume of proceedings, expensively priced and often poorly distributed, agencies should consider publishing proceedings as special issues in suitable journals. Agencies could also consider underwriting costs of special issues which, because of concentration on a theme, have the possibility of substantial single-copy sales. Agencies can also help by buying three-year subscriptions of selected ASEAN journals which can then be distributed to important academic institutions in other parts of the Third World.

7. Ensure that Third World books and journals are listed in major periodical and bibliographic directories; seek reviews of books in such journals as *Choice, Library Journal,* the *Times Literary Supplement,* and trade periodicals like *Publishers Weekly* and *The Bookseller.* The newsletters of scholarly societies should be tapped as well, but access is difficult and it may be necessary to buy advertising space.

For Southeast Asian scholarship to have the international impact it deserves, books and journals must reach the West. Southeast Asian publishers also need this crucial export market for purely commercial reasons. Yet it is important to retain perspective. If Southeast Asian publishers look too much toward export sales, decisions about what books can be published, and thus even the orientation of scholarship, may be influenced by perceptions of what will attract publishers in the industrialized nations. The main responsibility of scholarly publishers in Southeast Asia is to advance knowledge and contribute to the development of research in the region—not to serve an external market. They must also be aware that trends and funding change rapidly, and what may be a flourishing export market today may disappear tomorrow. Indeed, the market for Third World books in North America declined by an estimated 40 percent during the 1970s and is only now picking up again.

For Southeast Asia, the export of academic books is important, for it is difficult to support scholarly publishing fully on the local base. A market for books in English exists—not only in North America but in Australia, Japan, Britain, and, to a more limited extent, Western Europe. Consortia, cooperative efforts, creative marketing, and a detailed knowledge of overseas markets are crucial. Pioneering efforts have already been made, and the experiences of other Third World areas may be useful. Equally important will be the understanding and assistance of the western intellectual community in the interests of equitable scholarly exchange.

Epilogue

Knowledge Networks in the Modern World

The dissemination of knowledge is an increasingly complex phenomenon in the contemporary world. It involves many interrelated elements—the individual researcher or scholar who produces knowledge, the invisible college of peers who may assist in the creation or who provide commentary and evaluation, the mechanisms of publication such as journals, book publishers, and others, the libraries, and increasingly participants based on the new technologies, such as data bases and reprographic agencies. Users of knowledge may be based in academic institutions, government, industry or the general public. The ways in which users obtain access to knowledge is also varied. Knowledge is also international in scope and worldwide networks are involved. In short, even the distribution of specialized knowledge in the sciences requires an array of diverse instrumentalities. In order to understand the dissemination system in the modern world it is necessary to include economic, sociological, anthropological and perhaps even political perspectives.

A POLITICAL ECONOMY OF KNOWLEDGE DISSEMINATION

The creation and distribution of knowledge requires economic resources that, in many ways, determine how knowledge is used and who has access to it. The political economy of dissemination has domestic and international implications. Decisions concerning the funding of scientific research and, of course, the nature and facilities of the universities and other research institutions determine the base of knowledge production. Without an adequate institutional base and an appropriate and well-trained cadre of personnel, it is impossible to engage in the research and scholarship necessary for knowledge production in most fields. This fact means that many countries, which lack a minimum institutional base cannot compete and are left without the means of knowledge creation. This is the case for most of the Third World, where universities and research institutes are relatively new and where funds for research, libraries, and laboratories are limited. It is also true for many institutions of higher learning in the industrialized nations, that is, recently established universities or universities located in poorer parts of the country. Moreover, the smaller industrialized nations, such as Belgium and Switzerland, with highly developed academic institutions and long traditions of learning, are also at a considerable disadvantage because the size of their research system and the funds available are not large enough to permit effective participation with the major research powers.

There are several prerequisites for participating in the international research system. One, as noted above, relates to the size of the existing academic and research facilities and the ability to provide funding for research efforts. Another is a policy which stresses research as a priority. Such a policy direction not only includes government initiatives and funding for research, but also a climate in the academic and research communities that stresses productivity and publication. Research requires significant funding—and therefore governmental support. Only in a few countries, such as the United States, are nongovernment agencies such as foundations and industrial enterprises able to participate in sponsoring research. It is also necessary to have a sufficiently large number of scholars and researchers to undertake initiatives. Specialists in increasingly narrow fields are required to produce contemporary research.

By careful planning, it is possible for a country to build up research capability in limited areas. Malaysia, for example, does impressive research on rubber technology and is able to provide international leadership in this limited scientific area. The Philippines is now the leading country in rice research, in large part due to the International Rice Research Institute, which has funding from a number of countries and agencies but which is located in the Philippines. It is also possible for countries to build up a few internationally ranked universities which can participate in the international knowledge network. The Indian Institutes of Technology, for example, are involved in research of an international standard, and their academic programs are recognized for their high quality.

Not only is the production system fairly constrained and limited, but so too is the dissemination apparatus. The major journals, publishers, and distributors are located in a handful of countries. These tend to dominate the international flow of knowledge. They set the standard for scholarship and research and are the major "gatekeepers" of quality. At the present time, English functions as the major language of scholarship and research, and this dominance places nations which do not use English as a medium of communication at a disadvantage. Not only are the production and distribution facilities centered in a few countries, but the substantive decision-making apparatus for publishing is also similarly concentrated. The United States and Britain are the dominant forces in the distribution of scholarly and research knowledge. Most of the major journals are located in these two countries, as are the most important publishers. Concomitantly, most of the decisionmakers for knowledge distribution—the editors of books and journals, the academic evaluators of articles and manuscripts and the like—are located in these countries. It is, of course, an open system, and research materials are published in many countries. For example, countries such as the Netherlands, West Germany, and Sweden are now publishing materials in English to fully participate in the international knowledge system. And many countries have an active scholarly life of their own. Thus the dissemination of knowledge occurs in many languages and in many countries, but there is still a clear domination by the major English-speaking powers. It is probably fair to say that while there is an active scientific publication system in many countries, the international network is highly concentrated.

The market for scholarly and research materials is also part of an international system, and helps to determine the nature of the network. The major purchasers of scholarly materials are the libraries—mainly the academic and research libraries. Libraries account for about 80 percent of the sales of scholarly books and, in most fields, about 90 percent of the journals in the United States. Proportions in other countries are similar. And the library market is dominated by the North American and Western European academic and institutional libraries. This fact means that a publisher of books or journals must have access to these library markets to be successful. Academic books and journals in languages other than English can succeed without the major English-language library markets, of course, but it is sometimes more difficult to do so. And scholarly publications from a country like India can be successful by relying mainly on the Indian market because of a fairly large internal library market and relatively low costs for publishing. But Indian books rarely get into the international marketplace and therefore have less impact and a smaller potential circulation. It is virtually impossible for a knowledge dissemination system to be successful without a large, active, and relatively affluent library system in the universities to purchase the products of the scholarly publishers and journals.

Purchasers of books and journals depend on information to make their decisions. Thus the technology of publicity for books is an important part of the network. Bibliographical controls are an important element; in the United States, the Library of Congress, *Books in Print,* and several other bibliographical resources permit librarians and scholars to have easy access to information about current publication. In addition, publishers have access to individual scholars and relevant institutions through sophisticated computer-generated mailing lists. Journals feature reviews of new books and academic associations provide information about new publications. Other major industrialized nations have similarly rich bibliographical resources.

The academic "have-nots" do not have easy access to this system. Foreign publications are not easily included in the system. Overseas publishers are not attuned to using it. Virtually all Third World nations and many smaller industrialized nations have only rudimentary bibliographical resources, and thus have problems in distributing publications internally and have little access to the international network. On the commercial side, the apparatuses in the major industrialized nations dominate the international book trade and even have a strong influence in many smaller nations, both industrialized and Third World. The multinational book publishers have a crucial international role in both publishing and distributing books worldwide. Key British and French publishers retain a role in Third World nations which were formerly colonies. Longmans, Hachette, and Heinemann, to name only a few, are still important in a number of Third World countries. In the postwar era, American publishers have also entered the Third World book trade. The multinationals also operate in the industrialized nations. For example, the Dutch publisher Elsevier now has an important role in American scholarly publishing, as does Pergamon Press of Britain. But it is very difficult for the smaller Third World publishers to get international access to a market dominated by the multinational giants. Local publishers, of course, have a role in their own countries and can frequently effectively compete within a limited market with the multinationals. Access to bibliographical networks, to international markets, and to the prestige hierarchy of publishing remains very difficult for publishers from the peripheries.

There is an interrelationship in the knowledge network that is related not only to publishing, but also to the other complex elements of the system. The facilities for producing research and scholarship are related to the means of publishing the results, of effectively distributing publications, and of marketing books and journals. There has been no multifaceted analysis of the role of the entire knowledge system and its relevance to the roles of various countries and academic communities in this system. It is necessary to look at the various aspects of what can be called the "political economy" of knowledge distribution to fully understand the many ramifications of the system. Journal editing and publishing do not stand alone; they are part of the an interrelated system of knowledge.

TECHNOLOGY

Much has been said about the impact of the new technologies on publishing and knowledge distribution. Technological developments are very much part of the political economy of the system and must be understood in that context. What is a helpful technological innovation in one country may be a threat to the very existence of the publishing apparatus in another. One thing is clear: the development and production of most of the technological innovations in knowledge dissemination have taken place in the industrialized nations of the West and have worked to the advantage of the producers. Some have claimed that new technologies will permit "have-nots" to "leap-frog" into the world of twenty-first century knowledge distribution. While it is true that photo-offset printing has permitted countries which had no printing industry to quickly produce books, in general the major technological innovations have worked to the advantage of the major knowledge producers. For example, the growth of data bases which can provide quick access to major bibliographic resources has meant that nonmetropolitan countries which can afford access to the satellite-transmitted data bases can obtain services quickly. Yet the knowledge distributed through the data bases is focused on the needs of the major users—the large academic systems of the industrialized West—and the material included in them is almost exclusively from those systems. Moreover, control remains in the hands of the owners of the data bases—increasingly, profit-making Western information conglomerates. This aspect of technology further binds the users to the international knowledge and research system dominated by the Western industrialized nations, particularly the United States and Britain. While it provides quick access to information, it contributes in some ways to dependency and for the most part does not permit knowledge from the nonmetropolitan systems to be included in the system.

Other technological developments are more benign. The spread of reprography around the world, for example, has meant that some Third World nations can obtain access to imported books inexpensively by simply copying them. The combination of reprographic technology with photo-offset printing has permitted widespread piracy of books in many Third World nations. It has also permitted the users of knowledge to obtain access without the expensive and often cumbersome process of securing permissions from Western publishers or journals. Western publishing interests are naturally disturbed by the rise of piracy and the unbridled use of reprographic techniques in the Third World as well as in their own countries and steps have been taken to ensure compliance with the copyright laws. In 1986, for example, massive pressure from American and British publishing interests, including the threat of trade restrictions as well as legal action, forced Singapore, an active pirate of recorded tapes, films and computer software, to pass a stiff copyright law that will at least restrict the widespread piracy.

Photo-offset printing, by no means a new technology but nonetheless an important innovation of the past several decades, has meant that "short run" scholarly publishers throughout the world can economically publish books with limited circulation. The economics of academic publishing has been altered by a combination of photo-offset printing and computer-assisted typesetting. As the scientific community has demanded ever more specialized books for smaller audiences of experts, the new publishing technologies have permitted this demand to be met economically. Even in the United States, with its high labor costs, it is now possible to profitably publish an academic monograph with a printing of under 500, assuming that care is taken to control costs.

Photo-offset printing is also well entrenched throughout the world and has permitted considerable change in book publishing. The current expansion of "desktop publishing" both in the industrialized nations and in the Third World constitutes a potentially very important development as well. For around $20,000 it is possible to produce book-quality composed material ready for printing on an inexpensive photo-offset press. Small scale publishing, by combining computer assisted typesetting with photo-offset printing has significantly reduced the cost of producing short-run books and journals. This innovation also brings publishing within the realm of possibility for many academic and other institutions in the Third World. The Agricultural University of Malaysia, for example, makes use of such equipment successfully.

Thus, technology seems to have several implications for international knowledge distribution. On the one hand, relatively "low tech" innovations have been quite important in assisting academic and scientific publishing to develop. In high-cost countries, such as the United States and Britain, short-run academic publishing is commercially viable because of these innovations. In the Third World, the innovations have permitted the establishment of a specialized publishing industry at relatively low cost, despite the fact that most of the new machinery must be imported. The most advanced technologies, such as data-bases, high-speed printing and innovations using mainframe computers, have remained centralized in the industrialized nations and are likely to work against the decentralization of knowledge production and dissemination.

Many, including Marshall McLuhan, have argued that the world is moving away from a print-based knowledge and information system. The development of data bases, on-line computer information system, and even on-line journals in some specialized scientific fields seems to point in new technological directions. Libraries may be transformed by the newest innovation, the use of laser disks for storing information. Despite these changes, the traditional print-based books and journals seem to be well entrenched. They remain the cheapest means of communicating information. Furthermore, they are accepted by most users as the "legitimate" way of transmitting scholarship. At least in the social sciences and humanities, there is no real need to dramatically speed up knowledge dissemination. Traditional books and journals are readily accessible to individuals in all parts of the world and do not require any equipment to use. Thus, while the new technologies are transforming aspects of the knowledge system and will have long term implications for the ways in which information is produced and stored, it is also true that the traditional means of communicating—books and journals—are not about to become obsolete. Indeed, what seems to be occurring is the use of technological innovations—from reprography to computer-based typesetting—are being used to more efficiently and cheaply produce traditional books and journals.

THE INVISIBLE COLLEGE

Little is known about how the producers and users of knowledge interact with the publishing, distribution, and library systems that produce and make knowledge available. There has been some research in the sociology of science on research communities, patterns of scientific productivity, and the like, and there has been some analysis of the technical aspects of publishing. But few have explored how the networks of producers and distributors fit together. Scientific knowledge is produced in many locales, but academic institutions and research centers are at the center of the network. Universities provide the institutional framework, but informal groups of scholars are at the heart of the enterprise. The academic culture, where it supports research and scholarship, provides impetus. And funds are important to permit research in many fields. So too is the existence of libraries and laboratories to support research. But the invisible college of scholars is crucial. Most academic fields or disciplines have an informal network and also a hierarchy. Frequently, this network is international in scope. The invisible college has concrete reality in many ways. Periodic meetings and conferences permit scholars in a specific fields to engage in informal discussion. Conferences permit networks to expand, develop, and when a field has grown too large, perhaps bifurcate.

Scholarly journals are the most visible form of the invisible college. They have many informal functions. They provide a legitimation of knowledge by the decisions that are made on what to print. In this sense, the editors are key gatekeepers who in many ways control access to the field. Journals also permit relatively speedy communication of new knowledge to everyone involved in the network, and to those outside the structures as well. In many fields, there is a pecking order of journals, with those at the top of the prestige hierarchy having the most influence. Invisible colleges have institutional forms that are important for knowledge creation and distribution. Professional organizations in a field plan meetings and circulate information. The journals, sometimes affiliated with the scholarly organizations but frequently sponsored by publishing houses, are also a key institutionalization of the network. In some fields, book or monograph series also play a role in communication and legitimation. Those who stand at the center of any of these communication or publication systems have considerable power. They are in a way the leaders of the invisible colleges, having been placed in those positions of prestige and authority by their peers. While most scholarly leaders also hold chairs or other positions in major academic institutions or research organizations, their roles as leaders in the invisible college are for the most part informal and unremunerated.

The invisible college has important international implications. In most fields, scholarship is international and key leaders come from many countries. But as with the knowledge dissemination network discussed earlier, there are considerable imbalances in the system. Today's invisible colleges, in most fields of knowledge, are dominated by the metropolitan universities in the Western industrialized nations, particularly by North America and Britain. The key journals are published in these locations. The main evaluators, journal editors, publishing advisors, and other influential scholars are located in the major universities of the West. And as noted earlier, the network functions mainly in English. Scholars in peripheral institutions have little access to the mainstream and find it difficult to keep fully informed and up to date. They are simply not included in the informal networks and are frequently unaware of the latest developments and trends. Third World researchers are at a particular disadvantage because they are not only distant from the centers of scholarly power, but they frequently lack the resources to fully participate in the knowledge system of the invisible colleges. They usually cannot participate in international conferences, sometimes cannot afford to subscribe to the main journals in the field, and have little personal contact with the leaders in the field. Since their research facilities are often poorly equipped, they cannot participate at the forefront of current research. Library resources are also limited, so again the most recent information is unavailable.

Invisible colleges are frequently powerful cliques of scholars at the metropolitan institutions. These groups control virtually all the means of communication in a field and sometimes monopolize access. The publishers usually rely on the leaders in a field to make the basic decisions about what to publish, and these leaders, in turn, usually rely on their peers for advice. Thus the network is sometimes closed to outside development, often to the detriment of new ideas and developments. When a field becomes too moribund because of narrow or outdated leadership, alternative loci of development sometimes spring up, creating competing invisible colleges. This process is a complicated one, and it is often difficult for the knowledge network to adjust to such bifurcations in a field.

Because invisible colleges are not institutionalized, they are sometimes difficult to discern. This situation creates special problems for publishers and others involved in the dissemination network. In fact, publishers sometimes create a sense of organization in a field by sponsoring a journal and locating editors and advisors. In this way they may stimulate intellectual development. They certainly pave the way for giving visibility to the academic leaders in a field of study. Their choices are particularly important because their journals may become the main institutional loci for communication. The publishers are not in a position to judge among competing groups in a field, and they are frequently forced to make choices without having full access to the entire network. While it is true that to some extent scientific fields develop—and sometimes disappear—on their own, the knowledge dissemination network plays a very important role in determining the nature and focus of fields of study through the creation of journals, the sponsorship of book or monograph series, and the appointment of editors and advisors. In a very direct way, therefore, publishers make the invisible college visible. Their products are the legitimation of scholarship—perhaps the tip of the iceberg of scientific creativity.

ACCESS TO KNOWLEDGE NETWORKS

There are several kinds of access to knowledge networks, and each helps to determine the role and function of a scientific community. Elements of the knowledge dissemination apparatus are involved in all aspects of access. If research and scholarship are produced, they must be reported so that their results can be evaluated, assessed, and used by the relevant communities. Occasionally, the results of research—for example, public opinion polls or discoveries of cures for diseases—are disseminated widely in society. For the most part, however, research is communicated to smaller audiences of specialists or users. As noted earlier, researchers in the metropolitan centers have relatively easy access to the networks of dissemination. The journals, publishers, and data bases are readily at hand. Scholars, involved in any case at the forefront of their fields, use the latest paradigms and are aware of current debates in their field. They write in the dominant international languages. Researchers and scholars who work far from the center have a more difficult time obtaining access to the knowledge dissemination system. They sometimes do not use the metropolitan languages. Even when they do, they are frequently unaware of current debates and may not have the latest literature available to them. The invisible college of key scholars and decisionmakers in a field is far away—it may not even be clear where the centers of influence are located or what the key journals in a field are at a given time. Scholars at the peripheries are at a distinct disadvantage in gaining access to the means of communicating information to the major networks. If the research is done in a Third World country, it is even more difficult to obtain access to the international networks, since the disadvantages described here are magnified by lack of financial resources, considerable physical distances, lack of up-to-date library and laboratory facilities, and the like.

It might be argued that researchers do not necessarily need access to the international network and that science can proceed in a local framework. To some extent this is true, but most local or even national scientific communities are too small to provide the critiques, evaluations, and debates about research in specific fields necessary for a sustained and sophisticated scientific development. There is a need to participate in international communications networks and be involved with the mainstream of research. It is the case, for example, that even in research areas that have direct and applied relevance to Third World countries, such as rubber research in Southeast Asia, where impressive research facilities have been developed and good research is carried out, that scholars must be aware of currents in related scientific fields elsewhere. Where scientific work is conducted through local languages or even world languages (such as Chinese) which are not effectively part of the knowledge network, researchers are at a further disadvantage. Their work is simply not noticed and does not become part of the international network. Indeed, the Japanese are currently making a concerted effort to translate research done in the Japanese language into English so that it can become part of the world scientific network. If Japan, as a major scientific power in its own right, feels this necessity, smaller scientific communities have an even greater attachment to the international scientific network. Moreover, research that is not published in a journal using one of the major metropolitan languages, preferably in one of the major countries, frequently does not get picked up by the major bibliographical citation services and does not become part of the scientific mainstream.

The emergence of data bases and of bibliographic tools such as the Science Citation Index (SCI) has become a major yet unexamined force in the international knowledge network. SCI covers a large number of journals from many countries but is fairly weak for Third World journals and very deficient concerning journals published in non-Western languages. If the journal does not have a contents page in a Western language, it is not included in the SCI data base. SCI is widely used by scholars searching for materials in their fields. It is also used as a means of assessing the influence of particular research publications. Although it is a private corporation in the United States, its impact on measuring scientific productivity is very significant worldwide. Data bases are an even more problematic means of access to knowledge networks. They are almost exclusively developed in the major industrialized nations with materials largely from sources in the West. There are a few exceptions, such as the International Bureau of Education's (IBE) international data base for education, which consciously tries to use materials from a wide variety of countries, but even the IBE is largely limited to the official languages of the United Nations. The technology for data base development is expensive and largely limited to the Western countries at this time. It is also quite expensive to prepare and maintain a data base, and many are in fact built up by profit-making corporations, which charge substantial fees. Data base use also depends on access to computer and telecommunications networks, which virtually excludes many Third World countries.

Access is a multifaceted problem. On the one hand, it is necessary to be able to "input" to the network by publishing and including one's work in appropriate journals, bibliographies, and data bases. On the other hand, it is important to be able to use the existing networks, and this fact means that libraries, computer terminals, and involvement in the invisible college are of major importance. But access to these facilities is unequally available. The major metropolitan universities and the scholars working in them have easy access, while less important institutions in the industrialized nations have less access. Scholars working in most of the Third World find it very difficult to obtain access to these networks. Libraries find it difficult to keep up with current publications in many fields or have inadequate financial resources to purchase needed materials. Scholars do not find it easy to participate in international conferences and the other elements of the invisible college. Home institutions do not have funds to send them, or governmental restrictions do not permit easy travel. Uncertainties of mail service also limit quick access to informal networks on a continuing basis. Thus, Third World scientific communities are at a special disadvantage precisely because of their lack of access to virtualy all aspects of the international knowledge system. In the end, it is necessary to see access as an issue which has many ramifications and which lies at the heart of the knowledge system.

NORTH-SOUTH AND EAST-WEST

Debates concerning knowledge networks frequently focus on problems of North-South communication—the issue of more equal relationships between the industrialized North and the developing countries of the South. The issues are complex, involving as they do relationships between the major scientific and industrial centers and the Third World peripheries, many of which were until fairly recently under colonial domination. Some of UNESCO's proposals for changes in the communications networks have met with considerable opposition by the Western powers and contributed to the withdrawal of the United States from the organization. Without question, the relationship between the North and the South in terms of knowledge distribution is one of inequality. The nature of the inequalities is unquestioned, although the causes are widely debated. Under current conditions, it is unlikely that the patterns of inequality will dramatically change. Nevertheless, it is important to understand the nature of the system and to search for ways to ameliorate it.

Less analyzed are relationships between the industrialized market-economy nations of the West and the industrialized socialist nations of Eastern Europe and the Soviet Union, and between the Eastern Bloc countries and the Third World. The Soviet Union in most scientific fields, and several of the Eastern European nations in specific areas, are major scientific powers. Considerable research is produced. Scientific journals exist, and scholars are involved in research networks. Yet, in general, the Eastern European scientific community is not an integral part of the world scientific culture. Access to journals and books from Eastern Europe is difficult. These materials are not always part of data bases and bibliographies. Scholars are not regular participants in international scientific conferences and are not part of the invisible college.

Part of the problem is language. Russian is the dominant scientific language of Eastern Europe, although scholars in such countries as Hungary, the German Democratic Republic, and Poland frequently also use English or German as a means of communication. The major books and journals are either in Russian or in the Eastern European languages and thus do not have ready access to the international network. It is more common for Soviet or Eastern European scientists to know English or German than it is for Western scholars to know Russian. In many fields, there is a reluctance, especially in the Soviet Union, to share knowledge or even to permit journals free circulation outside the country. This attitude creates a closed scientific culture that does not welcome easy circulation with the outside world. The exchange of visits, so common in the invisible college of Western scholars, again is very difficult between East and West, although there are close scientific contacts within the Socialist Bloc. Direct government restrictions also apply; the Soviet authorities tightly control scientific interactions abroad a policy which makes spontaneous contacts are very difficult. Thus, for a number of reasons, the scientific system of Eastern Europe is in many ways a closed system that does not permit easy access. Soviet and Eastern European materials are seldom part of internationally used data bases. It also seems that scholars and scientists in Eastern Europe do not have easy access to publications and knowledge from the West and so have difficulty keeping abreast of current developments. Eastern scholars seldom contribute to the major international journals, although in some fields there is more interaction than in others. In the social sciences especially, there are severe limitations on East-West scholarly contacts and interactions.

A virtually unexplored aspect of the complex international equation are the scholarly interactions between the Socialist Bloc and the Third World. In some areas, there is considerable contact. For example, the Soviet Union, Czechoslovakia, and the German Democratic Republic are host to large numbers of foreign students. There are formal programs of interaction between scientists and scholars in the Soviet Union and a number of Third World nations—mostly those with close political ties to the USSR. The Soviet Union exports large numbers of books to the Third World in many languages, including university level textbooks, reference volumes, and scientific monographs of various kinds. All of these programs are means of maintaining contact with the Third World. Despite these efforts, however, it is clear that Eastern European scientific relations with the Third World are much weaker than those between the developing countries and the West. The exact nature of scientific interaction between the Socialist nations and the rest of the world deserves attention, since this major part of the world's scientific community is at present basically peripheral to the international system.

SOUTH-SOUTH RELATIONS

While most intellectual trade moves from North to South, with a balance of scientific payments heavily favoring the industrialized nations, there is a also a good deal of commerce among the developing countries of the Third World. It is significant that there is a significant flow of students to such Third World nations as India, the Philippines, and Mexico from other developing nations. India has been called the "research superpower" of the Third World, and it has some influence outside of own borders. Indian scientists are employed in many countries, Indian university-level textbooks are used in other parts of the Third World, and there is some attention paid to Indian scholarly journals. Regional networks also exist and are quite active. In Southeast Asia, for example, there is considerable formal and informal interaction among scientists and scholars, and organizations to foster further work are active. In Latin America, there are also close contacts, aided by the common use of Spanish.

Several Third World nations play a dominant role in their regions, in a way serving as regional centers for publishing, scholarship, and research. India, which continues to use English as its main language of scholarship and science and which has a large indigenous scientific community, plays a particularly important role in South Asia but also has some influence elsewhere in the Third World. In the Arabic-speaking world, Egypt has traditionally acted as an intellectual leader. Its universities train many students from other Arab countries, its journals are widely circulated in the region, and many Egyptian teachers work throughout the region. Latin America, Mexico, and Argentina, with their large academic systems and publishing enterprises, function as knowledge centers for Spanish-speaking Latin America. Thus it is evident that there is an active set of relations within the Third World. In some ways, the major knowledge powers, such as India or Egypt, function as centers within their regions and are somewhat resented by smaller countries.

But despite the relations that do exist, it is clear that the Third World relies on the West for most of its knowledge distribution. Traditional patterns of interaction based on the colonial past and the use of a European language, the foreign-aid policies of the industrialized nations, the location of the major journals and publishers and the domination of the invisible colleges by the West, the fact that many Third World scientists and scholars have been trained in the West and look to their alma maters for intellectual leadership, and other factors all contribute to continuing Western dominance of the knowledge system in the Third World. There are some signs of change, and the emergence of a regional consciousness is impressive. Yet it seems clear that the old relationships will continue for some time into the future.

In many ways, knowledge is power in the modern world. As many nations move toward an information-based, postindustrial society, knowledge and the means to create and distribute it become even more important. While in some ways the creation and distribution of knowledge are linked to existing institutions and facilities, such as well-endowed libraries, up-to-date research laboratories, and prestigious universities—meaning that those who control these infrastructures will have a significant advantage in the international knowledge network—it is easier to participate in the knowledge business than it is to develop, for example, heavy industry. By planning carefully and making enlightened choices, a country hitherto not involved can participate. Singapore, while by no means a knowledge superpower, is engaged in several ways in the international knowledge network. It has built up an impressive printing infrastructure and exports printed material worldwide. It also does its own scholarly publishing and does typesetting and printing for publishers in other countries. Several institutions have decided to specialize in areas that relate directly to Singapore's location and economic circumstances, and research is produced that is circulated internationally. Several scholarly journals from Singapore have a good deal of international status. In the industrialized world, the Netherlands, with a small academic and research base of its own, has become a major publisher of scholarly materials. Peripheral academic institutions, with the appropriate concentration of resources and with considerable planning, can move into the forefront of research, at least in some selected areas. The point is that participation in the international knowledge system does not require superpower status nor great wealth. Thus participation in the knowledge system may well offer countries or institutions now at the periphery an opportunity to participate in an increasingly important aspect of modern society with relatively little investment or dislocation.

It is necessary to carefully analyze the knowledge network in all its ramifications. Too often, those involved in publishing look only at the specific problems of the book industry, while librarians are concerned only with issues related to obtaining and storing materials. The academic community worries about research facilities, funds for scholarly work, and the nature of higher education. The fact is that all these elements, and more, are interrelated, and all impinge directly on the state of a nation's knowledge base. As has been noted, without a means for knowledge dissemination, the products of laboratories cannot get access to the international network. If the library system is small or underfunded, local publications—books and journals—will not have an adequate market. Thus the health of one part of the knowledge system directly affects other elements. There is truly an organic relationship among the various parts. Even if an institution or a nation cannot fully participate, it is nevertheless important to understand its place within the system, the options that may be available to it, and the costs and benefits of particular policies.

The knowledge network is complex. Those who currently dominate the network have considerable advantages. To a considerable extent, they control the copyright system, existing distribution networks, and the major international languages. Yet there is room for maneuver. A careful understanding of the nature of the network, the interrelationships of its elements, and the possibilities for independent action will yield not only understanding of one of the most important aspects of postindustrial society, but may also provide considerable autonomy.

Notes

Foreword

1. Philip G. Altbach, *Publishing in India: An Analysis* (Delhi and New York: Oxford University Press, 1975).

2. Philip G. Altbach and Eva Maria Rathgeber, *Publishing in the Third World: Trend Report and Bibliography* (New York: Praeger, 1980).

3. Philip G. Altbach, A. Arboleda, and S. Gopinathan, eds., *Publishing in the Third World: Knowledge and Development* (Portsmouth, N.H.: Heinemann, 1985).

4. Philip G. Altbach and Sheila McVey, eds., *Perspectives on Publishing* (Lexington, Mass.: Lexington Books, 1976).

Chapter 1

1. Many of the concepts elaborated in this chapter are taken from the writings of Edward Shils. See, particularly, *The Intellectuals and the Powers and Other Essays* Chicago: University of Chicago Press, 1972). See also Edward Shils, "Intellectuals," in *International Encyclopedia of the Social Sciences,* vol. 7 (New York: Macmillan 1968), pp. 399–415.

2. Chandler B. Grannis, "U.S. Book Industry Statistics," *Publishers Weekly* 205 (4 February 1974), p. 58. Statistics are for 1972.

3. For a general discussion of textbooks in the United States, see "Textbooks," in *Encyclopedia of Education,* vol. 9 (New York: Macmillan, 1971), pp. 210–224.

4. Grannis, "U.S. Book Industry Statistics," p. 58.

5. It might be noted that the United States has no equivalent to the *London Times Literary Supplement,* a publication which helps to set literary standards as well as to provide coverage of important new books.

6. For an overview of the book situation in the Third World, see Ronald Barker and Robert Escarpit, *The Book Hunger* (Paris: UNESCO, 1973).

7. See Edward Shils, "Metropolis and Province in the Intellectual Community," in Shils, *Intellectuals and the Powers,* pp. 355–371.

8. There are some exceptions to the use of copyright. See, for example, David Kaser, *Book Pirating in Taiwan* (Philadelphia: University of Pennsylvania Press, 1969).

9. *Records of the Conference for Revision of the Universal Copyright Convention* (Paris: UNESCO, 1973). See also N. N. Gidwani, ed., *Copyright: Legalized Piracy?* (Bombay: Indian Committee for Cultural Freedom, 1968).

10. See Datus C. Smith, Jr., *A Guide to Book Publishing* (New York: Bowker, 1966), for a brief discussion of the roles of the publisher.

11. Lewis A. Coser, "Publishers as Gatekeepers of Ideas," *Annals of the American Academy of Political and Social Science* 421 (September 1975), pp. 14–22. See also Paul M. Hirsch, "Processing Fads and Fashions: An Organization-Set Analysis of Cultural Industry Systems," *American Journal of Sociology* 77, no. 4 (1971), pp. 639–659, for a discussion of the intricacies of publishing and other cultural "industries."

12. Hirsch, "Processing Fads," p. 648.

13. See Sheila McVey, "Publishing in a Developing Country: America in the Nineteenth Century," *Annals of the American Academy of Political and Social Science* 421 (September 1975), pp. 67–80, for some examples of the situation in the United States.

14. See Edward Shils, "The Bookshop in America," *Daedalus* (Winter 1963), pp. 92–104, for a discussion of book selling in the United States.

15. Morris Philipson, "What Is a University Press Worth?" *Encounter* 40 (May 1973), p. 45.

16. It is probably true that in nations where the "intellectual infrastructure" is weak, the publisher is more important than in countries which have a system of television stations, intellectual journals, newspapers, and other outlets for knowledge.

17. John Dessauer, "Too Many Books?" *Publishers Weekly* 206 (30 September 1974 and 14 October 1974), pp. 24–25 and 32–33, respectively.

18. Barbara Ringer, "The Demonology of Copyright," *Publishers Weekly* 206 (18 November 1974), pp. 26–29.

Chapter 2

1. Barker and Escarpit, *The Book Hunger*, p. 16.

2. Ibid.

3. *Book Development in Asia: Report on the Production and Distribution of Books in the Region* (Paris: UNESCO, 1967), p. 25.

4. Latin America is an exception in this regard since either Spanish or Portuguese is the language of a great majority of the population and a large regional market for books exists. The two publishing giants of the region, Mexico and Argentina, have fairly effectively used this linguistic unity to build thriving publishing industries.

5. Edward Shils, *The Intellectual Between Tradition and Modernity: The Indian Situation* (The Hague: Mouton, 1963).

6. Smith, Jr., *Guide to Book Publishing.* See also Herbert Bailey, Jr., *The Art and Science of Book Publishing* (New York: Harper and Row, 1970).

7. Dan Lacy, "Practical Considerations, Including Financial, in the Creation, Production, and Distribution of Books and Other Educational Materials," in *The Mohonk Conference,* ed. Francis Keppel (New York: National Book Committee, 1973), pp. 55–66.

8. The developing countries are not alone in this situation, although it is much more serious where easy access to information and publications from abroad is lacking.

9. Tibor Mende, *From Aid to Recolonization: Lessons of a Failure* (New York: Pantheon, 1973).

10. John Nottingham, "Establishing an African Publishing Industry: A Study in Decolonization," *African Affairs* 68 (1969), pp. 139–144.

11. Donald McNeil, "International Book Programs of Major World Powers," in *American Books Abroad,* ed. William Childs and Donald McNeil (Washington, D.C.: Helen Dwight Reid Educational Foundation, 1986), p. 204.

12. Curtis Benjamin, *Books as Forces in National Development and International Relations* (New York: National Foreign Trade Council, 1964). See also Stanley Barnett and Roland Piggford, *Manual on Book and Library Activities in Developing Countries* (Washington, D.C.: Agency for International Development, 1969).

13. Ibid., p. 72.

14. An example of the possible effects of Western interpretations is the widespread notion of the key role of the middle classes in promoting stability and development in the Third World. Such a notion, while perhaps correct in some respects, fits neatly into the ideological predispositions and interests of American foreign policy, and has become, over the years, the dominant interpretation of American social science. While some scientists in the United States and in the Third World disagree with this interpretation, it has had a great influence on thinking in developing countries.

15. See Gidwani, *Copyright: Legalized Piracy?* See also Barker and Escarpit, *The Book Hunger,* pp. 88–102.

16. *Records of the Conference.*

17. See John Hawkins, *Education and Social Change in the People's Republic of China* (New York: Praeger, 1983).

Chapter 3

1. The author is indebted to Dr. Sheila Slaughter, Keith Smith, and Datus Smith, Jr., for their comments on an earlier draft of this chapter.

2. Don and Barbara Dodson, "Publishing Progress in Nigeria," *Scholarly Publishing* 4 (October 1972), p. 62.

3. This discussion is based on Altbach, *Publishing in India.*

4. See Arthur Isenberg, "Toward Better Book Distribution in Asian Countries," *Indian Book Industry* 2 (August–September 1970), pp. 35–55.

5. Ali Mazrui, *The Political Sociology of the English Language: An African Perspective* (The Hague: Mouton, 1975).

6. Keith Smith, "Who Controls Book Publishing in Anglophone Middle Africa?" *Annals of the American Academy of Political and Social Science* 421 (September 1975), pp. 140–150.

7. See Johann Galtung, "A Structural Theory of Imperialism," *African Review* 1 (April 1972), pp. 98–138; and Shils, *Intellectuals and the Powers.*

8. Philip G. Altbach, "Education and Neocolonialism," *Teachers College Record* 72 (May 1971), pp. 543–58.

9. Irwin Olian, Jr., "International Copyright and the Needs of Developing Countries," *Cornell International Law Journal* 7 (May 1974), pp. 81–112.

10. Nottingham, "Establishing an African Publishing Industry."

11. Printings of scholarly books are not dramatically larger in some industrialized nations—1,500 being a usual press run—but the editions tend to sell faster and the costing structure is often more favorable to the publisher.

12. See Edwina Oluwasnmi et al., eds., *Publishing in African in the Seventies* (Ile-Ife, Nigeria: University of Ife Press, 1975). See also Altbach, Arboleda, and Gopinathan, *Publishing in the Third World.*

13. See Gene Hawes, *To Advance Knowledge: A Handbook of American University Press Publishing* (New York: American University Press Services, 1967).

14. Chester Kerr, "Publishing Scholarly Books," in *Book Development: Some Current Problems,* ed. T. V. K. Krishnan (New Delhi: Federation of Publishers and Booksellers Associations in India, 1969), p. 126.

15. For current developments in African publishing, see issues of *African Book Publishing Record,* a journal published from Oxford, England.

16. For continuing reports concerning scholarly publishing in general and university presses in particular, see issues of *Scholarly Publishing.*

17. It should be noted in passing that books are not the only means of scholarly communications. For a discussion of journals, see chapter 8.

Chapter 4

1. Satish Saberwal, ed., *Towards a Cultural Policy* (New Delhi: Vikas, 1975).

2. For a further discussion of this concept, see Edward Shils, *Intellectuals and the Powers.*

3. See Anthony Smith, *The Geopolitics of Information: How Western Culture Dominates the World* (New York: Oxford University Press, 1980). See also Tunstall, *The Media are American* (London: Constable, 1977), pp. 116–125.

4. Tunstall, *The Media are American,* pp. 119–120.

5. A refreshing exception is Akhileshwar Jha, *Intellectuals at the Crossroads* (New Delhi: Vir, 1975), and from a different perspective, N. C. Chaudhury, *The Intellectual in India* (New Delhi: Vikas, 1977). For an Asian perspective, see S. H. Alatas, *Intellectuals in Developing Societies* (London: Cass, 1977).

6. See Jorg Becker, *The Geopolitics of Cultural Paper: International Dimensions of Paper Production* (Paris: UNESCO, 1982), for a general discussion of the problems of paper production and distribution.

7. Canada and Sweden are the world's major paper exporters and produce the largest quantities of wood pulp, the main ingredient of paper. Sweden has given large quantities of cultural paper to Third World nations as part of its foreign-aid program.

8. The classic discussion of the growth and development of the Indian film industry is Erick Barnouw and S. Krishnaswamy, *Indian Film* (New York: Columbia University Press, 1963).

9. For a broader discussion of the role of textbooks in the Third World, see chapter 7.

10. See also Krishna Kumar, ed., *Bonds Without Bondage: Explorations in Transcultural Interactions* (Honolulu: University Press of Hawaii, 1979).

11. It is significant that despite India's close political and military relationship with the Soviet Union, there is relatively little Soviet impact on education, the mass media, or the knowledge industry.

12. For a discussion of related issues in the Western context, see Richard Hoggart, *The Uses of Literacy* (New York: Oxford University Press, 1970).

13. See, for example, Gidwani, *Copyright: Legalized Piracy?,* and *International Copyright: Needs of Developing Countries* (New Delhi: Ministry of Education, 1967). For a broader view on copyright, see E. A. Olian, Jr., "International Copyright and the Needs of Developing Countries," *Cornell International Law Journal* 7 (May 1974), pp. 81–112.

14. This topic has been discussed at greater length in Philip G. Altbach, "Servitude of the Mind?" *Teachers College Record* 79 (December 1977), pp. 197–204.

Chapter 5

1. Altbach, "Servitude of the Mind?"

2. This chapter is based on longstanding concerns with the role of higher educational institutions in the development and distribution of knowledge. See Philip G. Altbach, "The Dilemma of Success: Universities in Advanced Develop-

ing Countries," *Prospects* 12, no. 3 (1982), pp. 293–312; and chapter 3. I am indebted to Lionel Lewis and Jeanne Weiler for their comments on an earlier draft of this chapter.

3. Joseph Ben-David has written extensively on the role of the university and its relationship to research. See his *Centers of Learning: Britain, France, Germany, United States* (New York: McGraw-Hill, 1977) and *Fundamental Research and the Universities: Some Comments on International Differences* (Paris: Organization for Economic Cooperation and Development, 1968).

4. Mary Biggs, ed., *Publishers and Librarians* (Chicago: University of Chicago Press, 1984).

5. Diana Crane, *Invisible Colleges: Diffusion of Knowledge in Scientific Communities* (Chicago: University of Chicago Press, 1972).

6. See James M. Kittelson and Pamel J. Transue, eds., *Rebirth, Reform and Resilience: Universities in Transition, 1300–1700* (Columbus, Ohio: Ohio State University Press, 1984); and Harold Perkin, "The Historical Perspective," in *Perspectives on Higher Education,* ed. Burton Clark (Berkeley, Calif.: University of California Press, 1984), pp. 17–55.

7. Laurence R. Veysey, *The Emergence of the American University* (Chicago: University of Chicago Press, 1965).

8. See Edward Shils, "Center and Periphery," in *Center and Periphery: Essays in Macrosociology* (Chicago: University of Chicago Press, 1975), pp. 3–16.

9. A. J. Engel, *From Clergyman to Don: The Rise of the Academic Profession in Nineteenth Century Oxford* (Oxford: Oxford University Press, 1983).

10. It is worth noting that the Soviet Union does not fully participate in the international knowledge network because of political constraints. This isolation is widely credited with limiting the development of science in the Soviet Union. China, during the Cultural Revolution, also turned its back on the outside world, and learned that isolation was not effective. Burma and Albania have pursued similar policies.

11. "English: Out to Conquer the World," *U.S. News and World Report* (18 February 1985), p. 50.

12. Louise Weinberg, "The Photocopying Revolution and the Copyright Crisis," *Public Interest* no. 38 (Winter 1975), pp. 99–110. See also Thomas R. Leavens, "In Defense of the Unauthorized Use: Recent Developments in Defending Copyright Infringement," *Law and Contemporary Problems* 44 (Autumn 1981), pp. 3–26.

13. Philip G. Altbach and Y. G. M. Lulat "International Students in Comparative Perspective: Toward a Political Economy of International Study," in *Research on Foreign Students and International Study: An Overview and Bibliography,* by P. G. Altbach, D. H. Kelly, and Y. Lulat (New York: Praeger, 1985), pp. 1–66.

14. Eugene Garfield, "Mapping Science in the Third World," *Science and Public Policy* 10 (June 1983), p. 114.

15. *Scholarly Communication: The Report of the National Enquiry* (Baltimore: Johns Hopkins University Press, 1979).

16. Eleanor Harman, ed., *The University as Publisher* (Toronto: University of Toronto Press, 1967).

17. Rush Welter, *Problems of Scholarly Publication in the Humanities and Social Sciences* (New York: American Council of Learned Societies, 1959). See also Chandler Grannis, "Scholarly Publishing," in *The Book Publishing Annual* (New York: Bowker, 1985), pp. 4–8.

18. Hawes, *To Advance Knowledge*.

19. Gregory Walker, *Soviet Book Publishing Policy* (Cambridge: Cambridge University Press, 1978).

20. *Scholarly Publishing,* a journal published by the University of Toronto Press, is the best means of following developments in scholarly publishing in general and among the university presses in particular.

21. Academic staff in the most prestigious universities seem to have better access to the key scholarly journals than those in undergraduate colleges or less research-oriented universities in the United States. There is greater stress on publication in these prestigious institutions. Thus, there are considerable variations in scholarly writing in the United States.

22. One exception to this happy relationship is the censorship of the *Chicago Review* by its academic sponsor over the issue of publishing writings of the Beat Generation. The "Beats" left the journal and started their own publication, *Big Table,* and the *Chicago Review* lost a place in literary history.

23. See Claude T. Bishop, *How to Edit a Scientific Journal* (Philadelphia: ISI Press, 1984), for a practical guide to the publication of academic journals.

24. For a perspective on Third World journal publishing, see chapter 8.

25. For an overview of journal usage, see Eugene Garfield, "Science in the Third World," *Science Age* (October–November, 1983), pp. 59–65. Garfield notes that few Third World countries produce journals that are widely used internationally. India is the only country that seems to have much impact.

26. Hassan Ali Al-Ebraheem and Richard P. Stevens, "Organization, Management and Academic Problems at an Arab University: The Kuwait University Experience," *Higher Education* 9 (March 1980), pp. 203–218.

27. Murray Ross, *The University: Anatomy of Academe* (New York: McGraw-Hill, 1976). See also Philip G. Altbach, *University Reform: An International Perspective* (Washington, D.C.: American Association for Higher Education, 1980).

28. Crane, *Invisible Colleges*.

29. See Walter W. Powell, *Getting Into Print: The Decision-Making Process in Scholarly Publishing* (Chicago: University of Chicago Press, 1985).

30. Don Swanson, ed., *The Role of Libraries in the Growth of Knowledge* (Chicago: University of Chicago Press, 1980).

31. Fritz Machlup and Kenneth Leeson, *Information Through the Printed Word;* vol. 2: *Journals* (New York: Praeger, 1978).

32. At least one major American university, the University of Wisconsin at Madison, completely stopped purchasing new books and journals for an extended period.

33. Machlup and Leeson, *Information Through the Printed Word;* volume 3: *Libraries* (New York: Praeger, 1978).

34. Edward Shils, *The Academic Ethic* (Chicago: University of Chicago Press, 1983).

Chapter 6

1. Weinberg, "The Photocopying Revolution," and Leavens, "In Defense of the Unauthorized Use."

2. Edward W. Ploman and L. Clark Hamilton, *Copyright: Intellectual Property in the Information Age* (London: Routledge and Kegan Paul, 1980), chapter 1.

3. See Ringer, "The Demonology of Copyright."

4. Ploman and Hamilton, *Copyright,* p. 123. For a broader perspective, see Walker, *Soviet Book Publishing Policy.*

5. Stephen Breyer, "The Uneasy Case for Copyright: A Study of Copyright in Books, Photocopies and Computer Programs," *Harvard Law Review* 84 (December 1970), p. 281. Breyer's is one of the best contemporary analyses of copyright, and his arguments are generally unsympathetic to copyright. See also William S. Strong, *The Copyright Book: A Practical Guide* (Cambridge, Mass.: MIT Press, 1981).

6. See Nicholas L. Henry, "Copyright, Public Policy and Information Technology," *Science,* no. 1983 (February 1974), pp. 384–391.

7. Edward Ploman, "Copyright: Where Do We Go From Here?" in Altbach, Arboleda, and Gopinathan, *Publishing in the Third World,* p. 27. Similar themes are discussed in Armand Mattelart, *Transnationals and the Third World: The Struggle for Culture* (South Hadley, Mass.: Bergin and Garvey, 1983), and Mattelart and Siegelaub, *Communication and Class Struggle.*

8. Olian, Jr., "International Copyright." See also Gavin McFarlane, *A Practical Introduction to Copyright* (London: McGraw-Hill, 1982), p. 100; and Jane Bortnick, "International Information Flow: The Developing World Perspective," *Cornell International Law Journal* 14 (Summer 1981), pp. 333–353.

9. Ploman, "Copyright," p. 26.

10. Lyman Patterson, *Copyright in Historical Perspective* (Nashville, Tenn.: Vanderbilt University Press, 1978), p. 222. See also R. F. Whale, *Copyright: Evolution, Theory and Practice* (London: Longmans, 1970).

11. Ian Parsons, "Copyright and Society," in A. Briggs, ed., *Essays in the History of Publishing* (London: Longmans, 1974), pp. 29–60.

12. Ibid., p. 32.

13. Dorothy M. Schrader, "Armageddon in International Copyright: Review of the Berne Convention, the Universal Convention and the Present Crisis in International Copyright," *Advances in Librarianship* 2 (1971), p. 309.

14. See Allan P. Cramer, "International Copyright and the Soviet Union," *Duke Law Journal* (1965) pp. 531–545; Herbert R. Lottman, "Inside VAAP," *Publishers Weekly* (8 September 1975), pp. 28–34; and Alan U. Schwartz, "Publishing Detente: The Time of the VAAP," *Publishers Weekly* (3 March 1975), pp. 28–31.

15. For a general elaboration of this point, see McVey. For a broader perspective, see Seymour Martin Lipset, *The First New Nation* (London: Heinemann, 1964).

16. Patterson, *Copyright in Historical Perspective*, p. 197.

17. John Tebbel, *A History of Book Publishing in the United States*, vol. 2 (New York: Bowker, 1975).

18. Barbara Ringer, "The Role of the United States in International Copyright: Past, Present and Future," *Georgetown Law Journal* 56 (1968), p. 1054.

19. Olian, Jr., "International Copyright," p. 93.

20. Ringer, "The Role of the United States," p. 1051.

21. *The ABC of Copyright* (Paris: UNESCO, 1981), p. 66. See also Ploman and Hamilton, *Copyright*.

22. Denis de Freitas, *The Copyright System: Practice and Problems in Developing Countries* (London: Commonwealth Secretariat, 1983), p. 5.

23. With the recent departure of both the United States and Great Britain from UNESCO, the future of the Universal Copyright Convention's administration is unclear, as is the important statistical work done by UNESCO in the field of books and copyright.

24. Ploman, "Copyright," p. 58.

25. T. S. Krishnamurthi, "Copyright: Another View," *Copyright Society of the USA Bulletin* 15 (April 1968), pp. 217–234.

26. *ABC of Copyright*, p. 69.

27. *International Copyright: Needs of Developing Countries* (New Delhi: Ministry of Education, Government of India, 1967). See also de Freitas, *The Copyright System*; Olian, Jr., "International Copyright"; and *Records of the Conference for Revision of the Universal Copyright Convention*, 5–24 July 1971 (Paris: UNESCO, 1973).

28. *ABC of Copyright*, p. 71.

29. de Freitas, *The Copyright System*, p. 61 ff.

30. R. E. Barker, "Copyright Concessions for the Developing Countries," *Bookseller*, no. 3364 (13 June 1970), pp. 2598–2602; and no. 3365 (20 June 1970), pp. 2678–2684.

31. Zachariah Chafee, Jr., "Reflections on the Law of Copyright-I," *Columbia Law Review* 45 (July 1945), pp. 503–529.

32. Parsons, "Copyright and Society."

33. For a broader discussion of these issues, see Altbach, "Servitude of the Mind?" See also Philip G. Altbach, "Literary Colonialism: Books in the Third World," *Harvard Educational Review* 45 (May 1976), pp. 226–236.

34. For further discussion of the implications of foreign study, see Philip G. Altbach, "The Foreign Student Dilemma," *Teachers College Records* 87 (Summer, 1986), pp. 589–610.

35. There are some significant, although as yet fairly minor, countertrends of some Third World nations building up an indigenous scientific capacity and using this capacity for local purposes. See S. Gopinathan, "Intellectual Dependency and the Indigenization Response: Case Studies of Three Disciplines in Two Third World Universities" (Ph.D. dissertation, State University of New York at Buffalo, 1984).

36. See Mazrui, *Political Sociology.* For a different perspective, see Randolph Quirk and H. G. Widdowson, eds., *English in the World: Teaching and Learning the Language and Literatures* (Cambridge: Cambridge University Press, 1985).

37. "English: Out to Conquer the World," p. 49.

38. Smith, "Who Controls Book Publishing?"

39. See Curtis G. Benjamin, *U.S. Books Abroad: Neglected Ambassadors* (Washington, D.C.: Library of Congress, 1984).

40. Becker, "The Geopolitics of Cultural Paper."

41. These controls are not only evident in the area of books and publishing, but also in such field as mass communications. See, for example, Jonathan Fenby, *The International News Services* (New York: Schocken Books, 1986); and Tunstall, *The Media are American.*

42. Shahid Alikhan, "The Problem of Piracy," in *International Publishing Today,* ed. O. P. Ghai and N. Kumar (Delhi: Bookman's Club, 1984), p. 55.

43. Kaser, *Book Pirating in Taiwan.* See also "In Taiwan, a Cool Look at the Courteous Pirates," *Bookseller,* no. 3358 (2 May 1970), pp. 2202–2206.

44. Macaulay, cited earlier (footnote 5), stresses the monopoly argument in his classic anticopyright treatise. See also Leavens, "In Defense of the Unauthorized Use"; and Breyer, "The Uneasy Case for Copyright."

45. Manuel E. Valdehuesa, Jr., "Need to Stop, Look and Listen: Copyright and Piracy at the 21st IPA Congress," *Asian Book Development* 12 (October 1980), p. 11.

46. Paul Nijhoff Asser, "Piracy, 2nd Part," *STM Newsletter* 53 (April 1980).

47. David Kaser states that more than 4,500 titles were pirated over a 20-year period in Taiwan. Kaser, *Book Pirating in Taiwan,* p. 123.

48. For two informative overviews, see Herbert I Schiller, *Who Knows? Information in the Age of the Fortune 500* (Norwood, N.J.: Ablex, 1981); and

Kaarle Nordenstreng and Herbert I. Schiller, eds., *National Sovereignty and International Communication* (Norwood, N.J.: Ablex, 1979).

49. Datus Smith, Jr., "The Bright Promise of Publishing in the Developing Countries," *Annals of the American Academic of Political and Social Science* 421 (September 1975), pp. 130–139.

50. See Susie Rodwell, "A World Communications Crisis?" *Compare* 15, no. 1 (1985), pp. 53–66.

51. Weinberg, "The Photocopying Revolution."

52. Nicholas Henry, *Copyright: Information Technology and Public Policy*, 2 vol. (New York: Marcel Dekker, 1975). See also David Ladd, "Copyright and the International Technologic Environment," *Copyright Bulletin* 17, no. 3 (1983), pp. 17–24.

53. It should be noted that similar issues related to the reproduction of video cassettes, tape recordings, and computer software are all related to the basic issues involved with the control of unauthorized copying of written material from books and journals. There is, if anything, more pressure on nonbook copying since the demand for such material is greater and the potential profits higher.

54. Leavens, "In Defense of Unauthorized Use."

55. Rita Cruise O'Brien, "Technological Factors in International Communication," *Communication* 5 (1980), pp. 89–106. See also Daniel Bell, "Communications Technology: For Better or For Worse," *Harvard Business Review* (May–June 1969), pp. 1–8.

56. See Stephen Heyneman, Joseph Farrell and M. Sepulveda-Sturado, *Textbooks and Achievement; What We Know* (Washington, D.C.: The World Bank, 1978). See also Susan Wagner, "Textbooks and Third World Education: The World Bank's Changing Role," *Publishers Weekly* 215 (26 March 1979), pp. 41–43.

57. See Altbach, *Publishing in India*.

58. David Ladd, "The Future of Copyright," *Publishers Weekly* 225 (1 June 1984), pp. 24–26.

59. Sean McBride, et al., *Many Voices, One World: Communication and Society Today and Tomorrow* (Paris: UNESCO, 1980). See also R. C. O'Brien and G. K. Helleiner, "The Political Economics of Information in a Changing National Order," *International Organization* 34, no. 4 (Autumn 1980), pp. 445–470.

Chapter 7

1. Heyneman, Farrell, and Sepulveda-Stuardo, *Textbooks and Achievement*.

2. See chapter 1.

3. International Development Research Center, *The World of Literacy: Policy, Research and Action* (Ottawa: IDRC, 1979).

4. Smith, "Who Controls Book Publishing?"

5. The educational heritage of colonialism is complex and, of course, not entirely one-sided. School policies were made by the colonizers but were often influenced by the colonized. For a broad discussion of the colonial impact on education, see Philip G. Altbach and Gall P. Kelly, *Education and the Colonial Experience.* (New Brunswick, N.J.: Transaction Books, 1984).

6. For a broader discussion of the role of the multinational corporations on knowledge distribution, see Smith, *The Geopolitics of Information.*

7. Smith, "Who Controls Book Publishing?"

8. See chapter 6.

9. See chapter 2.

10. See Smith, *Guide to Book Publishing.* See also F. Richardeau, *Conception et production des maneuls scolaires: Guide pratique* (Paris, UNESCO, 1979).

11. A recent trend in the United States is toward "managed texts," in which the editorial staff not only works with the writers but actually writes substantial parts of the book. See Phillip Whitten, "College Textbook Publishing in the 1970s," *Annals of the American Academy of Political and Social Science* 421 (May 1975), pp. 56–66.

Chapter 8

1. For a broader discussion of the international knowledge network, see Philip G. Altbach, "The Distribution of Knowledge in the Third World," in P. G. Altbach, *Higher Education in the Third World: Themes and Variations* (Singapore: Maruzen, 1982), pp. 85–106.

2. For a general discussion of the Third World publishing scene, see Altbach, Arboleda, and Gopinathan, *Publishing in the Third World.*

3. UNESCO statistics, for example, indicate that by far the largest amount of translation takes place from English to other languages. Thus English is the main source of knowledge that is desired by readers of other languages.

4. Currency fluctuations affect scholarly publishing and the distribution of knowledge. The cost of journals in the Third World has risen because of the current strength of the U.S. dollar.

5. See Miriam Balaban, ed., *Scientific Information Transfer: The Editor's Role* (Dordrecht, Holland: Riedel, 1978).

6. For a practical guide aimed at editors of Western academic journals, see Bishop, *How to Edit a Scientific Journal.*

7. For a Third World perspective on issues of intellectual independence, see Mazrui, "The African University."

Chapter 9

1. General issues of publishing in the Third World have been considered in Altbach, *Publishing in India*; and Philip G. Altbach and Keith Smith, "Publishing

in the Third World," *Library Trends* 26 (Spring 1978), pp. 449–600 (special issue).

2. This study is based largely on interviews with approximately fifty individuals directly involved with publishing in Maharashtra, a consideration of the limited literature available on the subject, and by interviews with Marathi publishers. Without the assistance of the Marathi publishing trade, this discussion would have been impossible. I am indebted to these busy individuals who freely gave of their time. I also appreciate the comments of Ramdas Bhatkal, Sadashiv Padhye, and Sheila Slaughter on an earlier draft.

3. See Smith, Jr., *Guide to Book Publishing*; and Barker and Escarpit, *The Book Hunger*, for detailed considerations of the problems of Third World publishing.

4. For further discussion of these matters, see Smith, "Who Controls Book Publishing?"

5. See Samuel Israel, "The Colonial Heritage in Indian Publishing," *Library Trends* 26 (Spring 1978), pp. 539–553; and Altbach, *Publishing in India*.

6. The only full discussion of the history of Marathi publishing is A. H. Limaye, *The Nature of Publications in Marathi: Motivation and Tradition* (Poona: Prasad Prakashan, 1972), in Marathi.

7. It should be noted in this regard that at least one Maharashtra government policy, the "nationalization" of school textbook production, removed a lucrative market for private-sector publishers and materially weakened the book trade in the state.

8. See Altbach, *Publishing in India*, pp. 48–53. See also Isenberg, "Toward Better Book Distribution."

9. Interview with P. C. Manaktala, Bombay, 8 October 1977.

10. The investment necessary for a book published in English would be about 25 percent higher because of higher overheads, a different discount structure, somewhat higher printing costs, and the use of more costly paper and binding.

11. For a discussion of the board's programs, see Maharashtra State Board for Literature and Culture, *Objectives, Programmes, Progress* (Bombay: Government of Maharashtra, 1976).

12. Interview with Kulkarni, Continental Prakashan, Poona, 10 October 1977.

13. See Walker, *Soviet Book Publishing Policy*.

14. See Bill Henderson, ed., *The Publish It Yourself Handbook: Literary Tradition and How-To* (Yonkers, N.Y.: Pushcart Book Press, 1973).

Chapter 10

1. For an elaboration of this point, see chapter 2.

2. There are some exceptions to this rule. Zed Books in London, for example, is devoted exclusively to publishing books from Third World perspectives for an international audience. The well-known African Writers Series of Heinemann Publishers has also done much to reflect Third World literature in an international context.

3. For an analysis of the African situation, see Keith Smith, "Books and Development in Africa: Access and Role," *Library Trends* 26 (Spring 1978), pp. 469–488.

4. For a revealing new study of editorial decision making in American scholarly publishing, see Powell, *Getting Into Print.*

5. See chapter 8.

6. Something of a countertrend can be seen in the decision of a publisher like Heinemann to concentrate on school texts in Southeast Asia and to slow its production of scholarly monographs. Texts are more profitable.

7. *Bookseller* (16 March 1975).

8. The Asia Foundation, *Annual Report 1982* (San Francisco, 1982).

9. P. G. Altbach and S. Gopinathan, "The Dilemma of Success: Higher Education in Advanced Developing Countries," in Altbach, *Higher Education in the Third World.*

10. S. Gopinathan, "Intellectual Dependency."

11. Datuk Hassan Ahmad, "The Role of the Dewan Bahasa dan Pustaka in the Advancement of Indigenous Academic Publishing in Malaysia," paper delivered at the Seminar on Academic Publishing in the ASEAN Region, Singapore, September 1985.

12. Data for this section are derived from country papers presented at the Seminar on Academic Publishing in the ASEAN Region, Singapore, September 1985.

13. For a recent account of the prospects and problems of journal publishing in Indonesia, see Salman Kasenda, "Academic Journals in Indonesia: Their Importance, Development and Problems," *RIHED Bulletin* 9, no. 4 (1982).

14. S. Gopinathan and J. Clammer, "English-Language Scholarly Journals in Singapore: A Profile and Commentary," paper presented at the Seminar on Academic Publishing in the ASEAN Region, Singapore, September 1985.

Index